[This book is intentionally blank!]

[This book is intentionally blank!]

[This book is intentionally blank!]

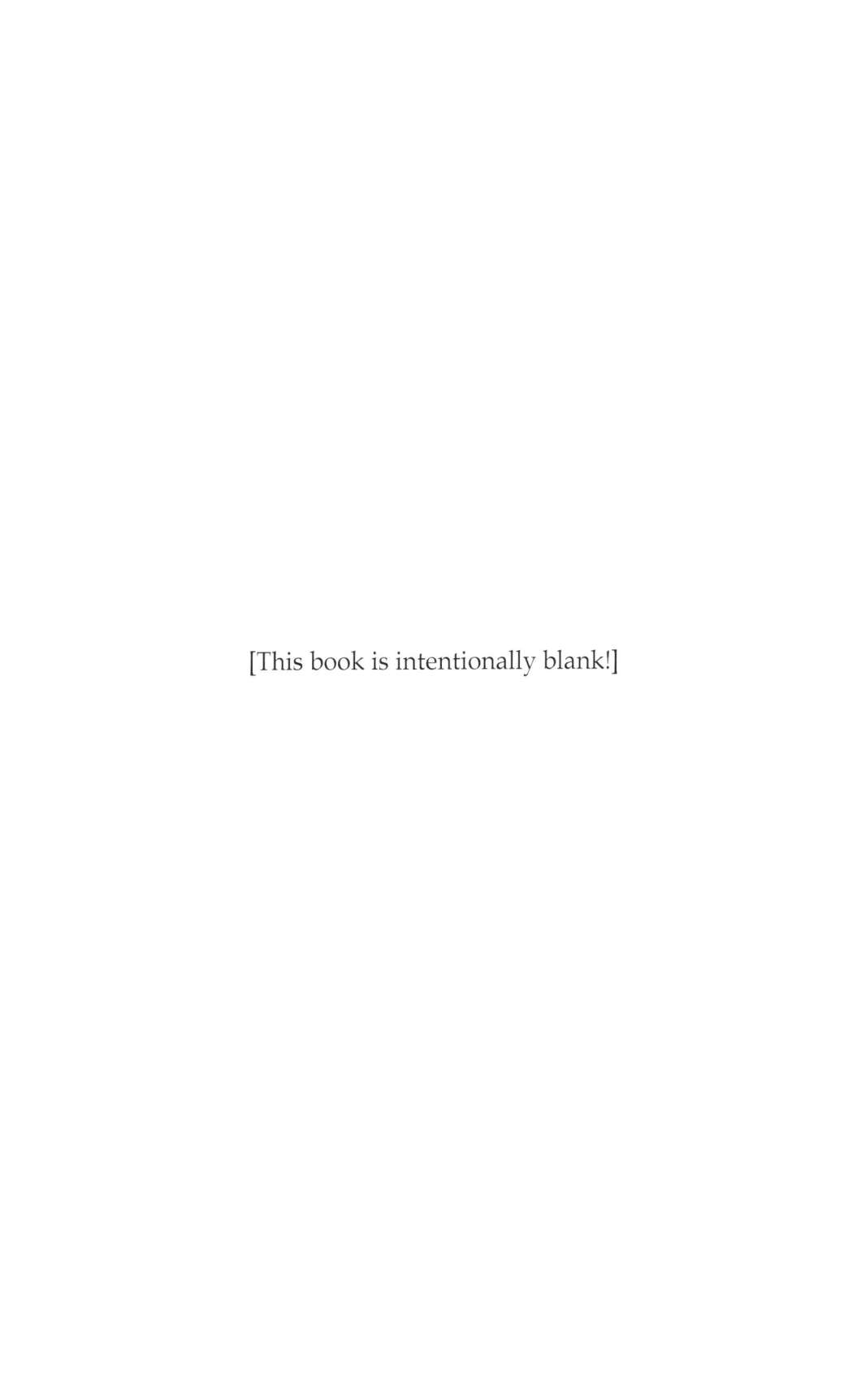

[This book is intentionally blank!]

[This book is intentionally blank!]

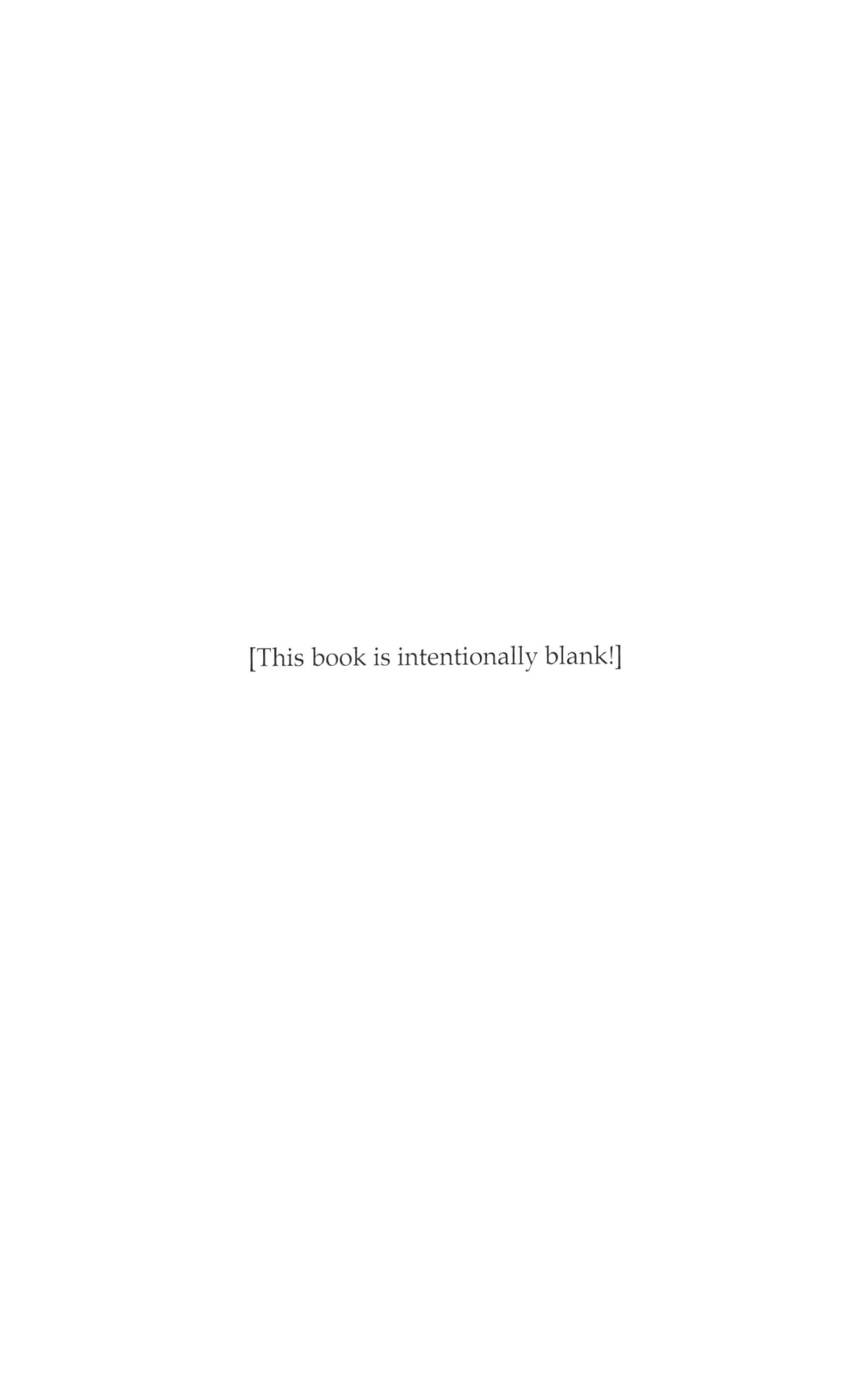

[This book is intentionally blank!]

[This book is intentionally blank!]

[This book is intentionally blank!]

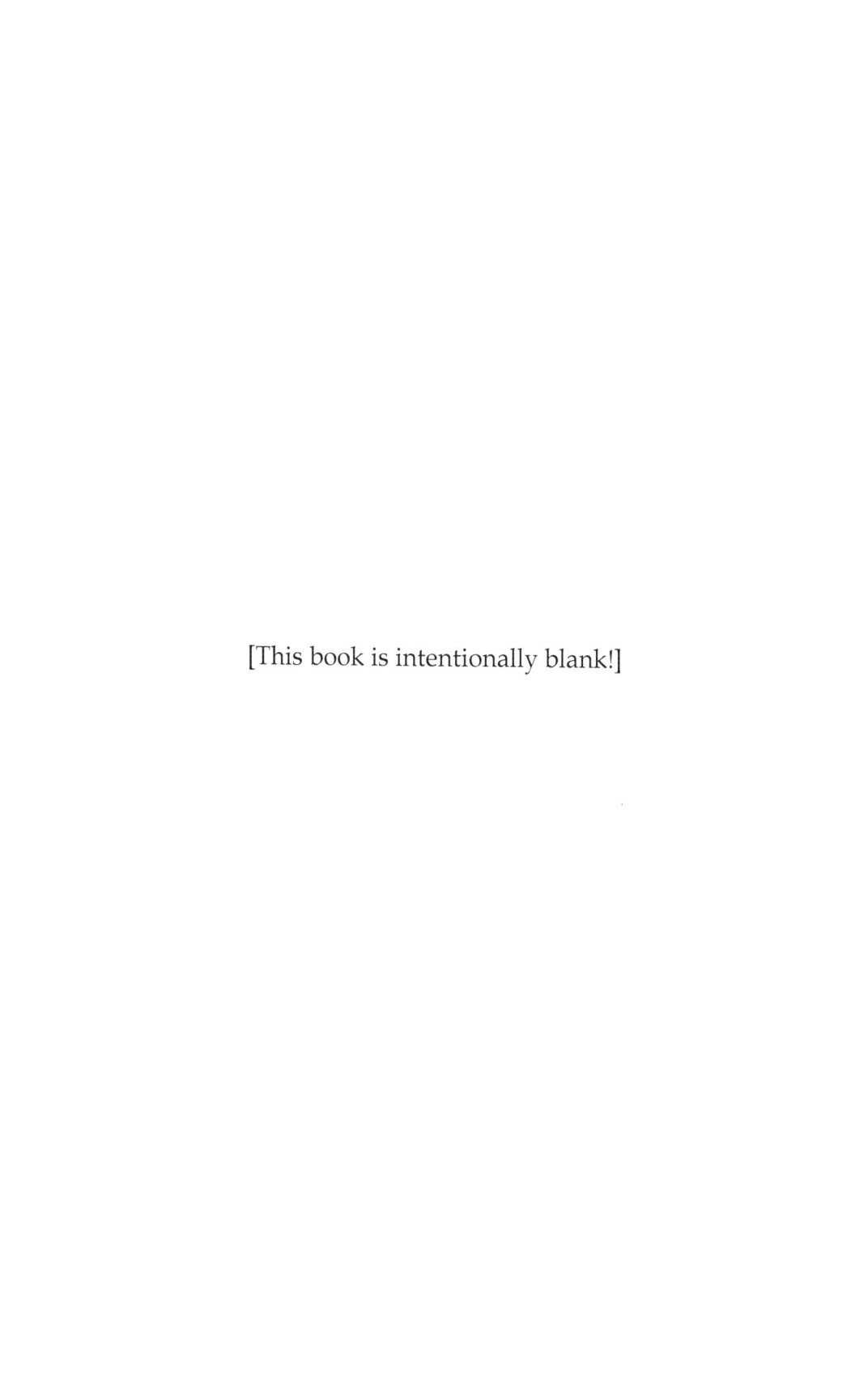

[This book is intentionally blank!]

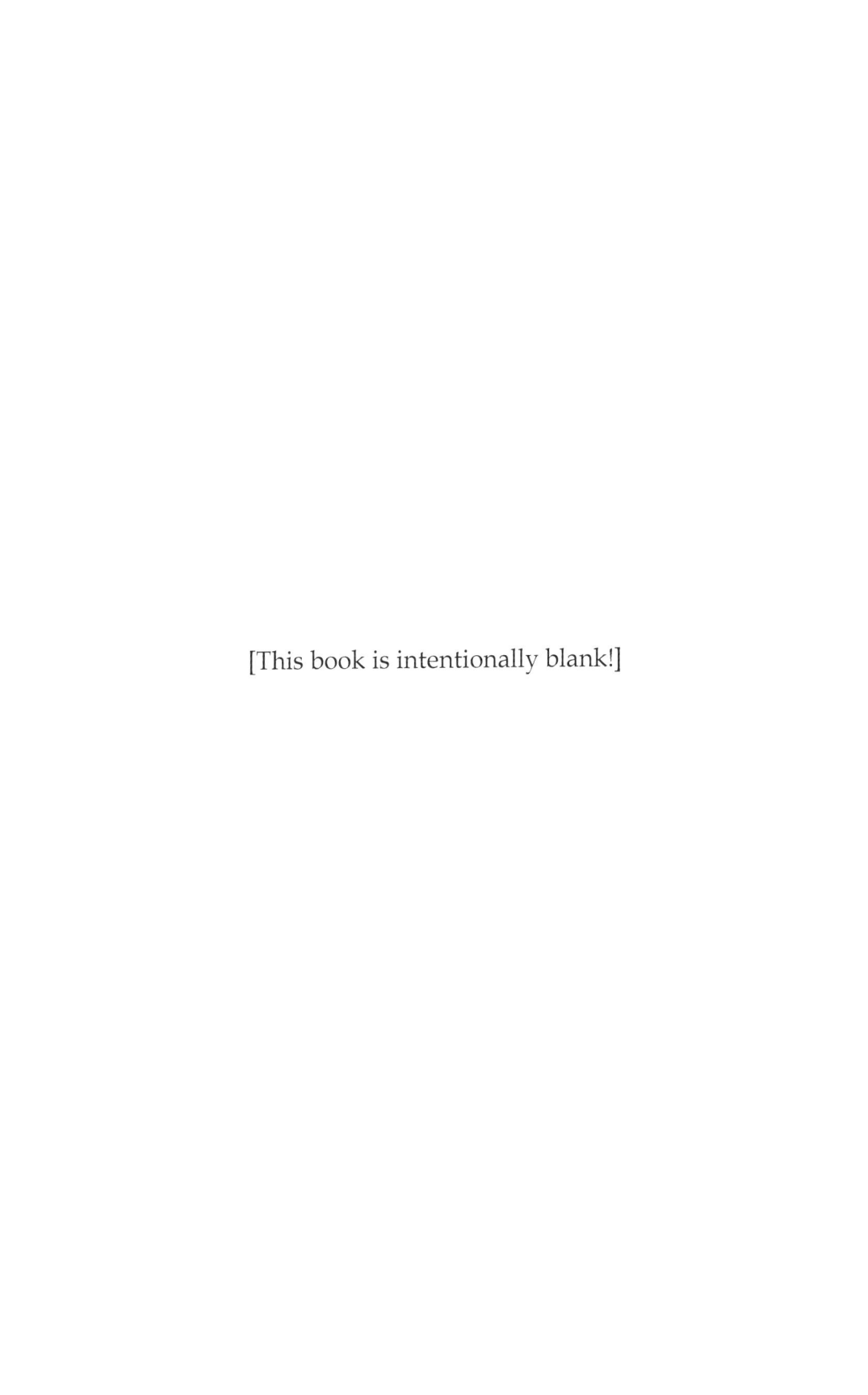

[This book is intentionally blank!]

[This book is intentionally blank!]

[This book is intentionally blank!]

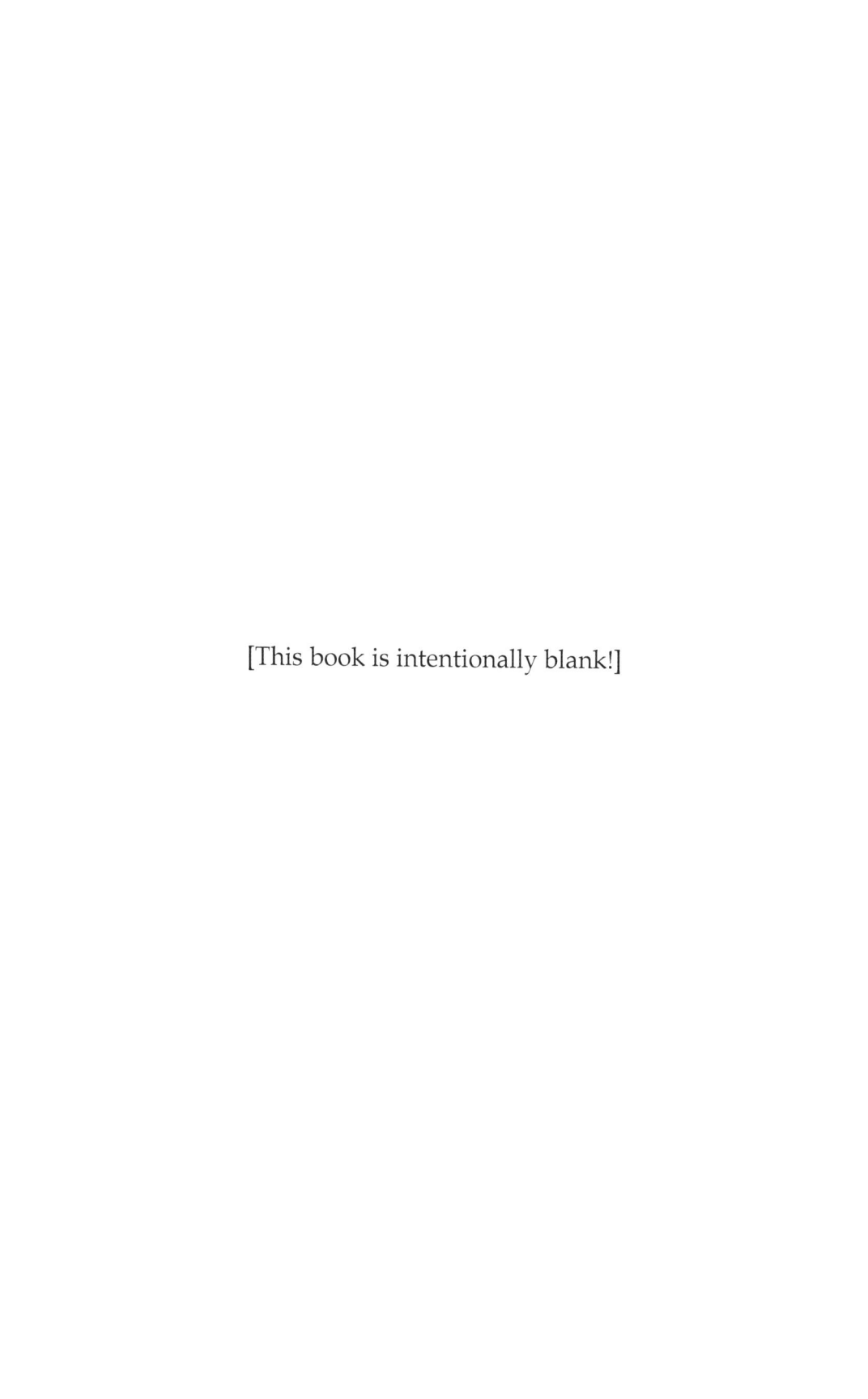

[This book is intentionally blank!]

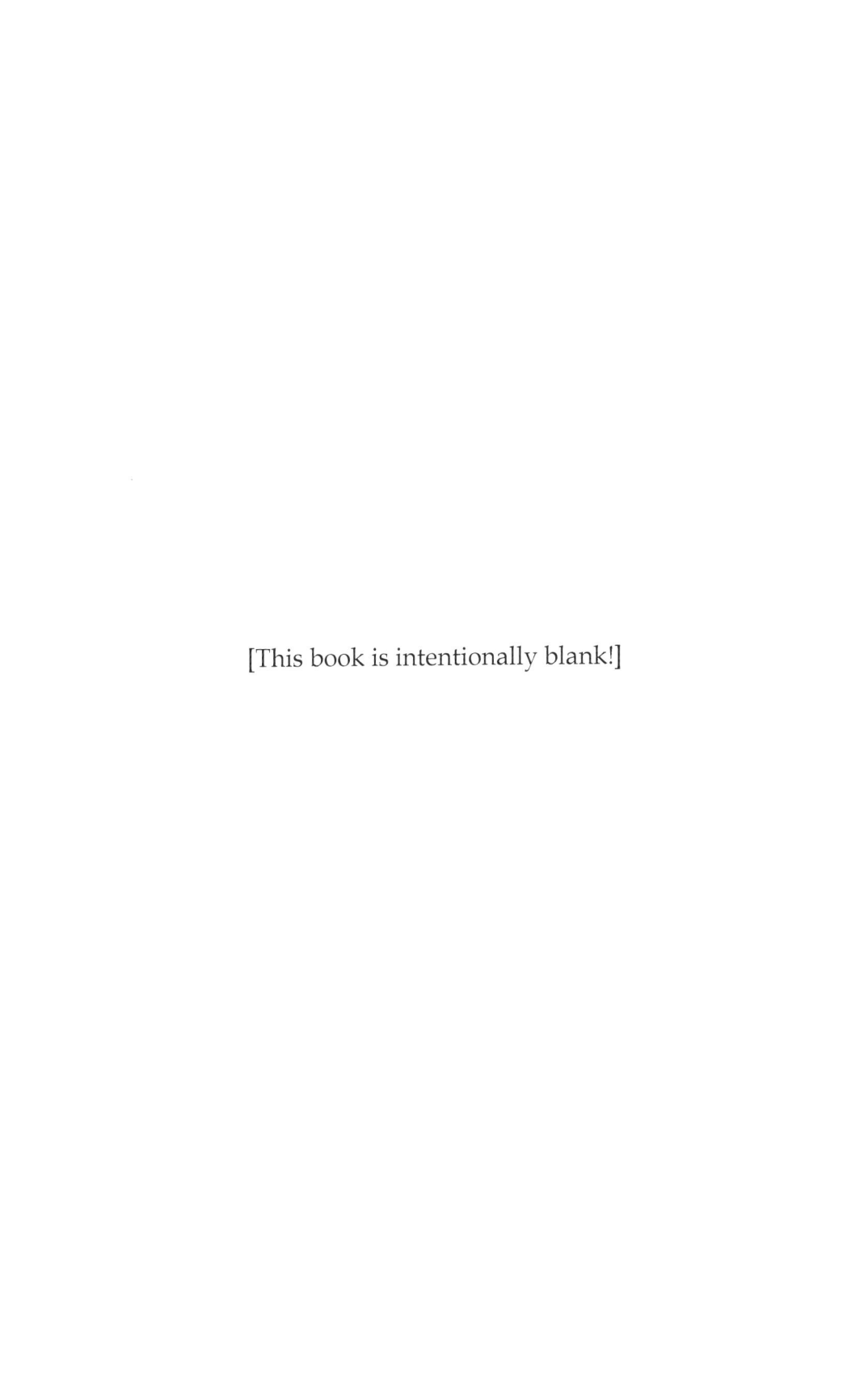

[This book is intentionally blank!]

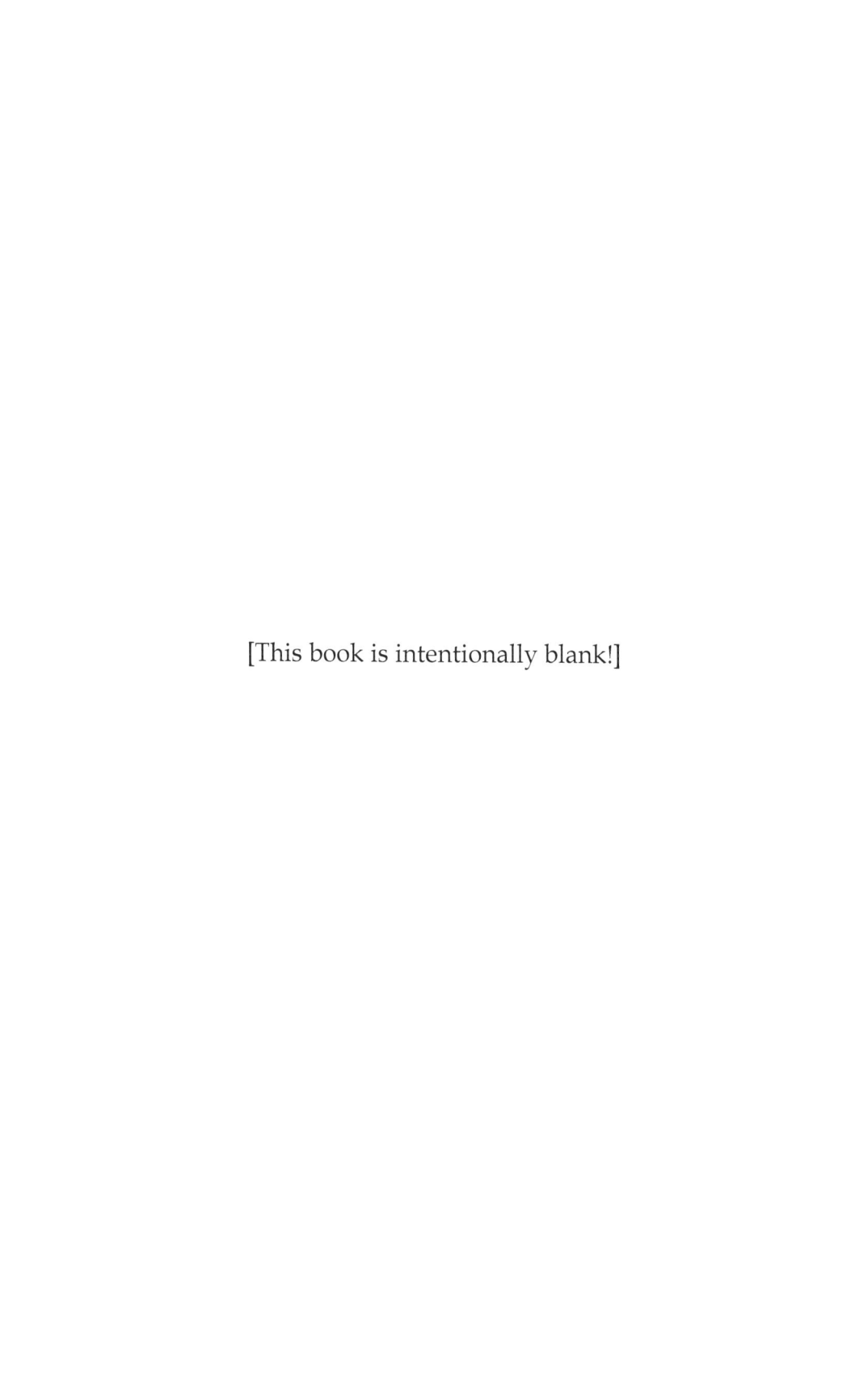

[This book is intentionally blank!]

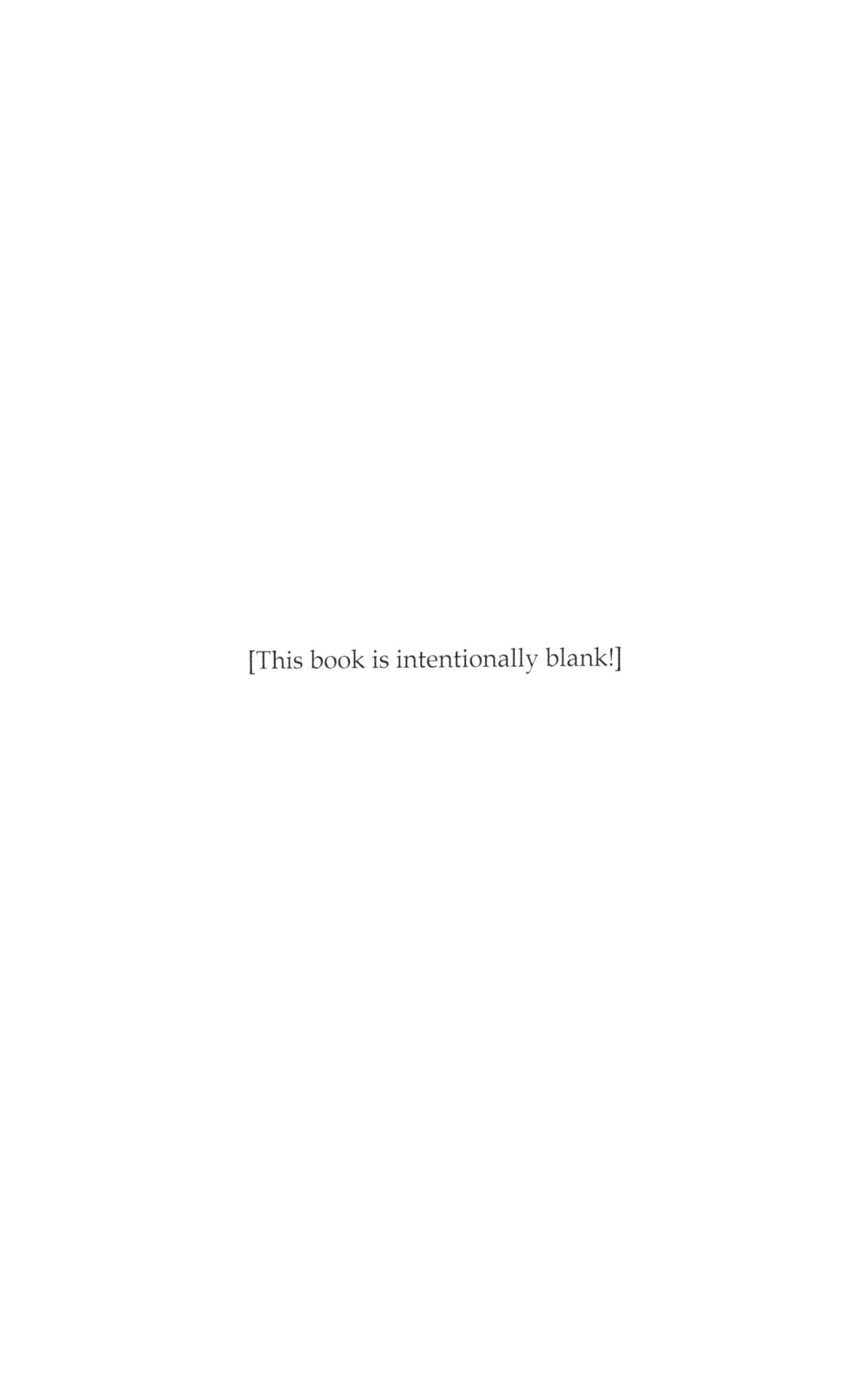

[This book is intentionally blank!]

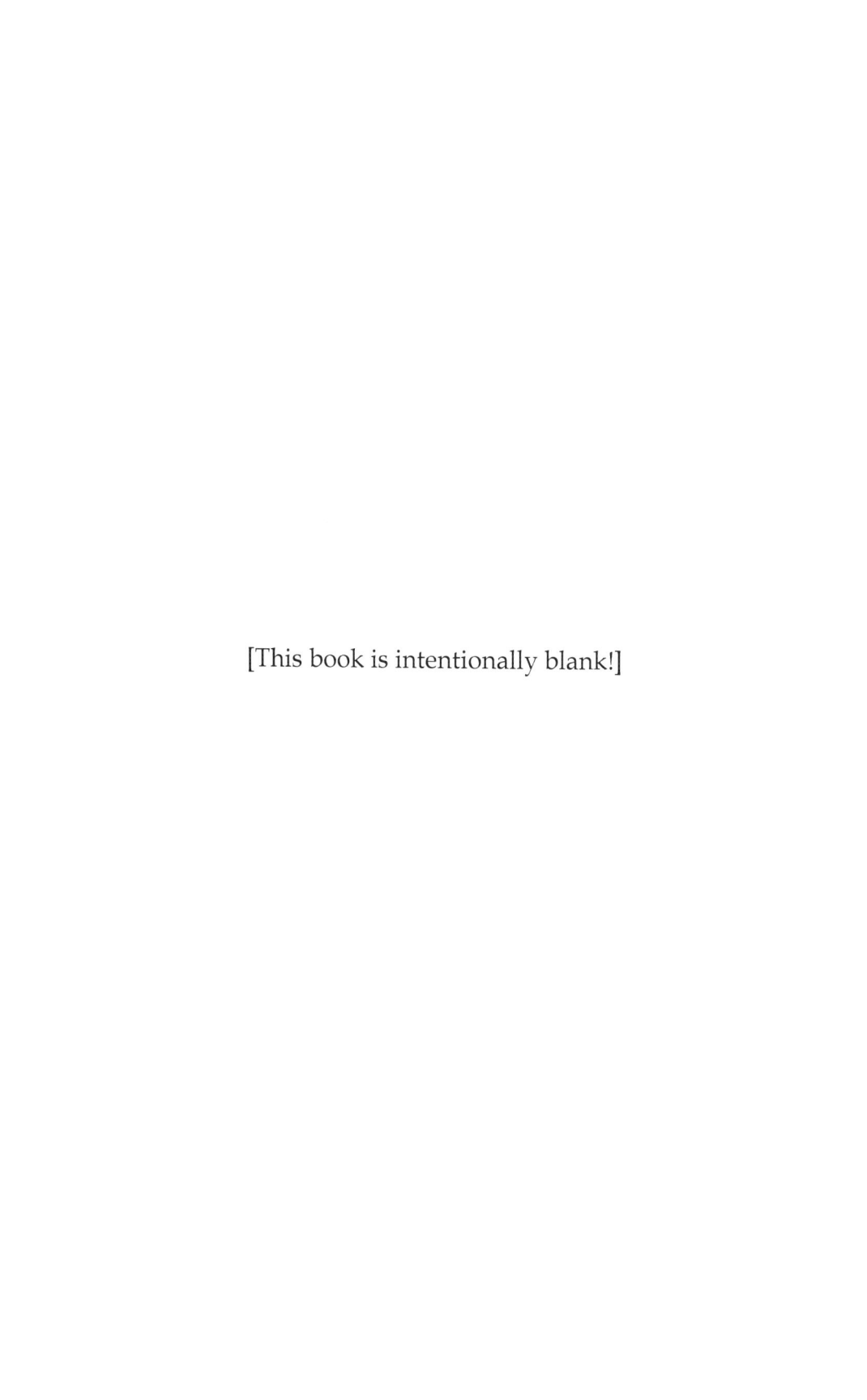

[This book is intentionally blank!]

[This book is intentionally blank!]

[This book is intentionally blank!]

[This book is intentionally blank!]

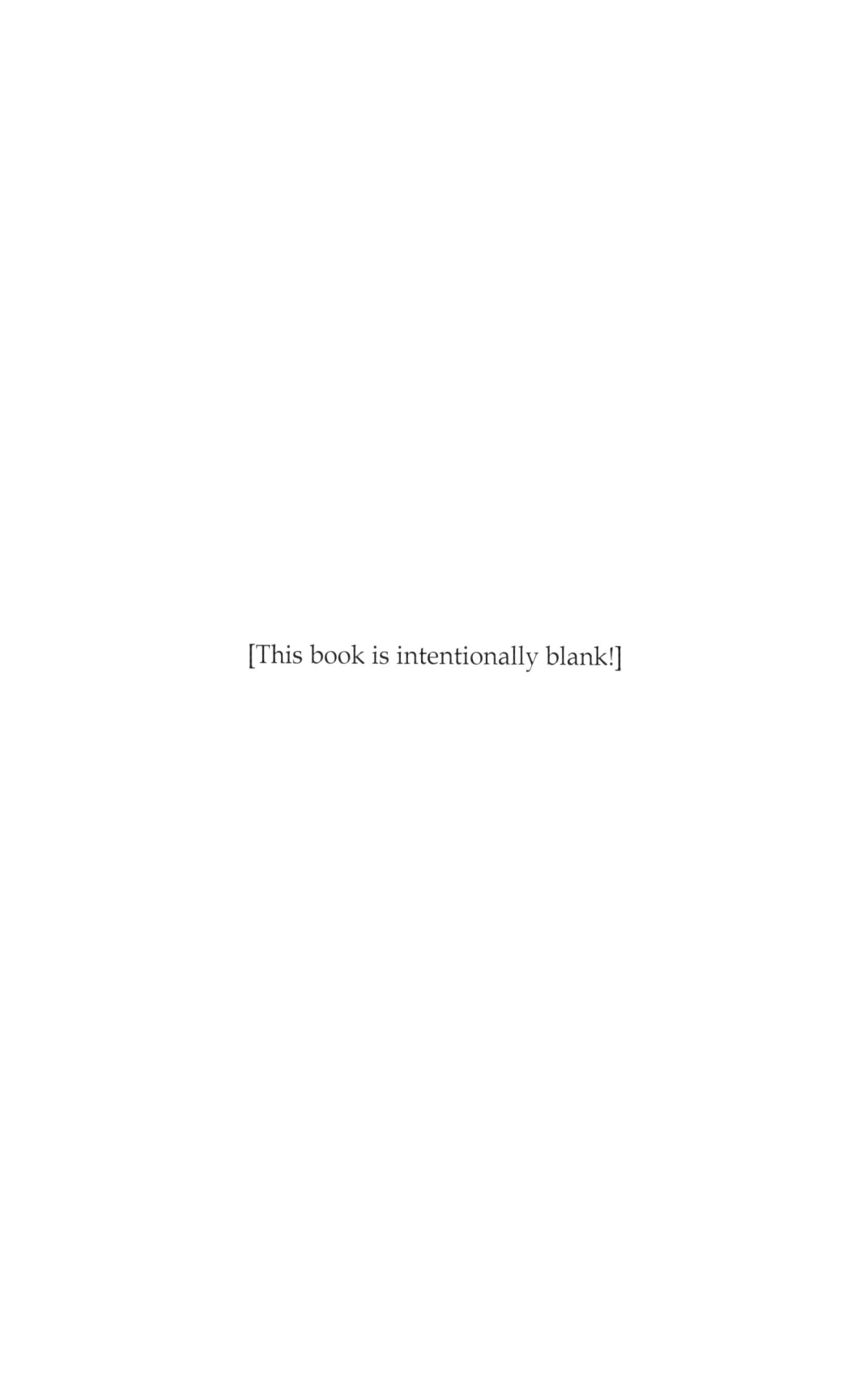

[This book is intentionally blank!]

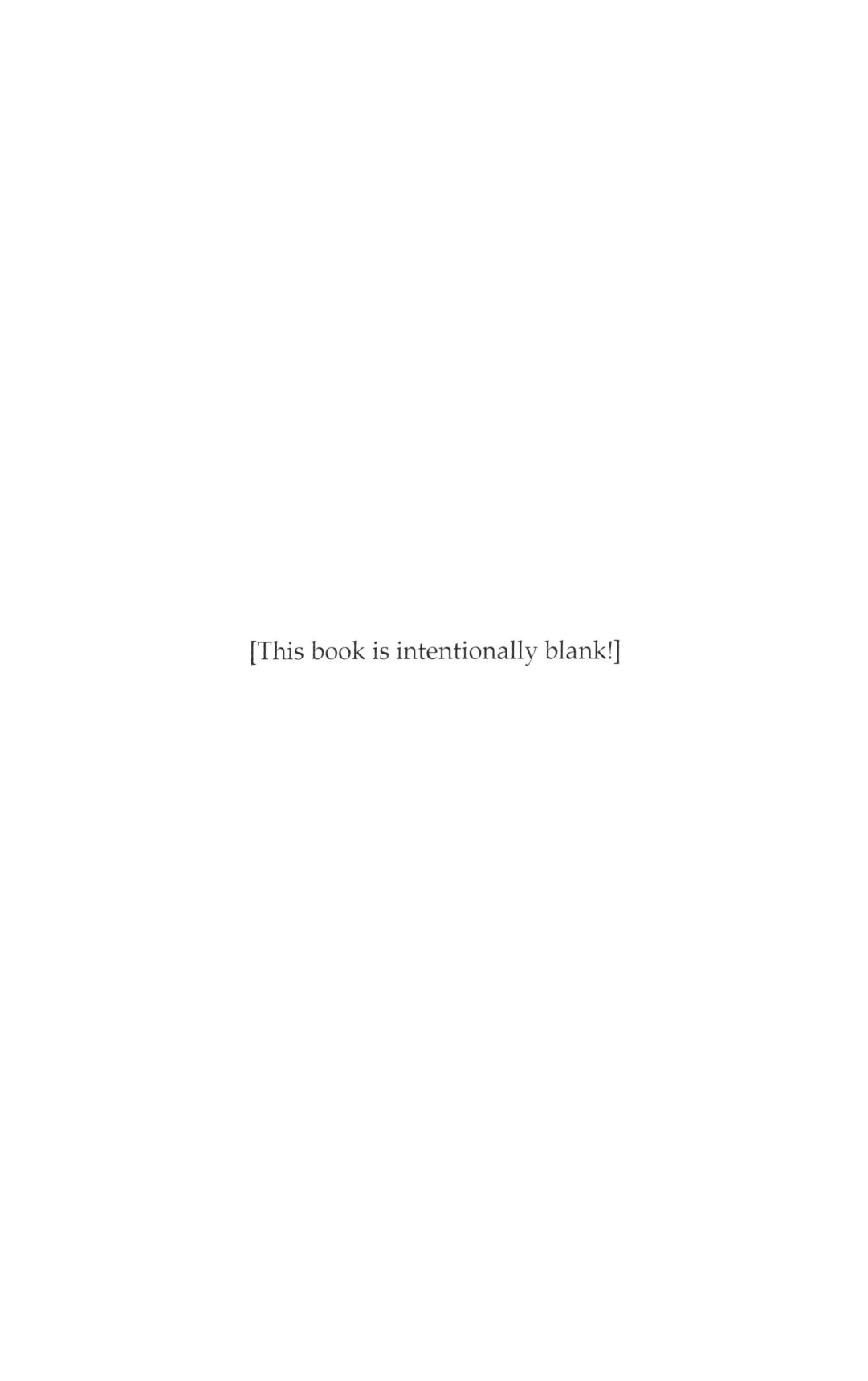

[This book is intentionally blank!]

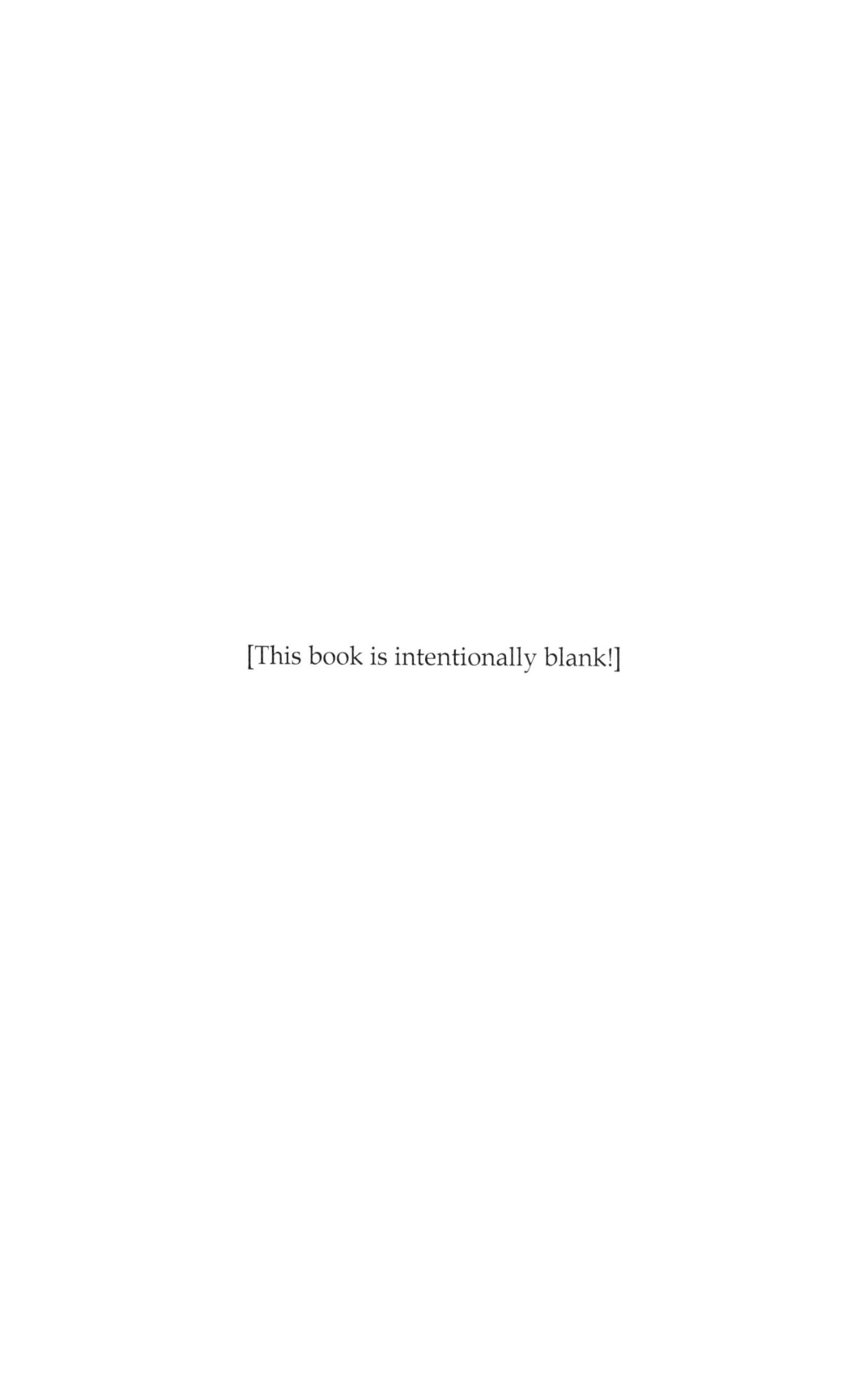

[This book is intentionally blank!]

[This book is intentionally blank!]

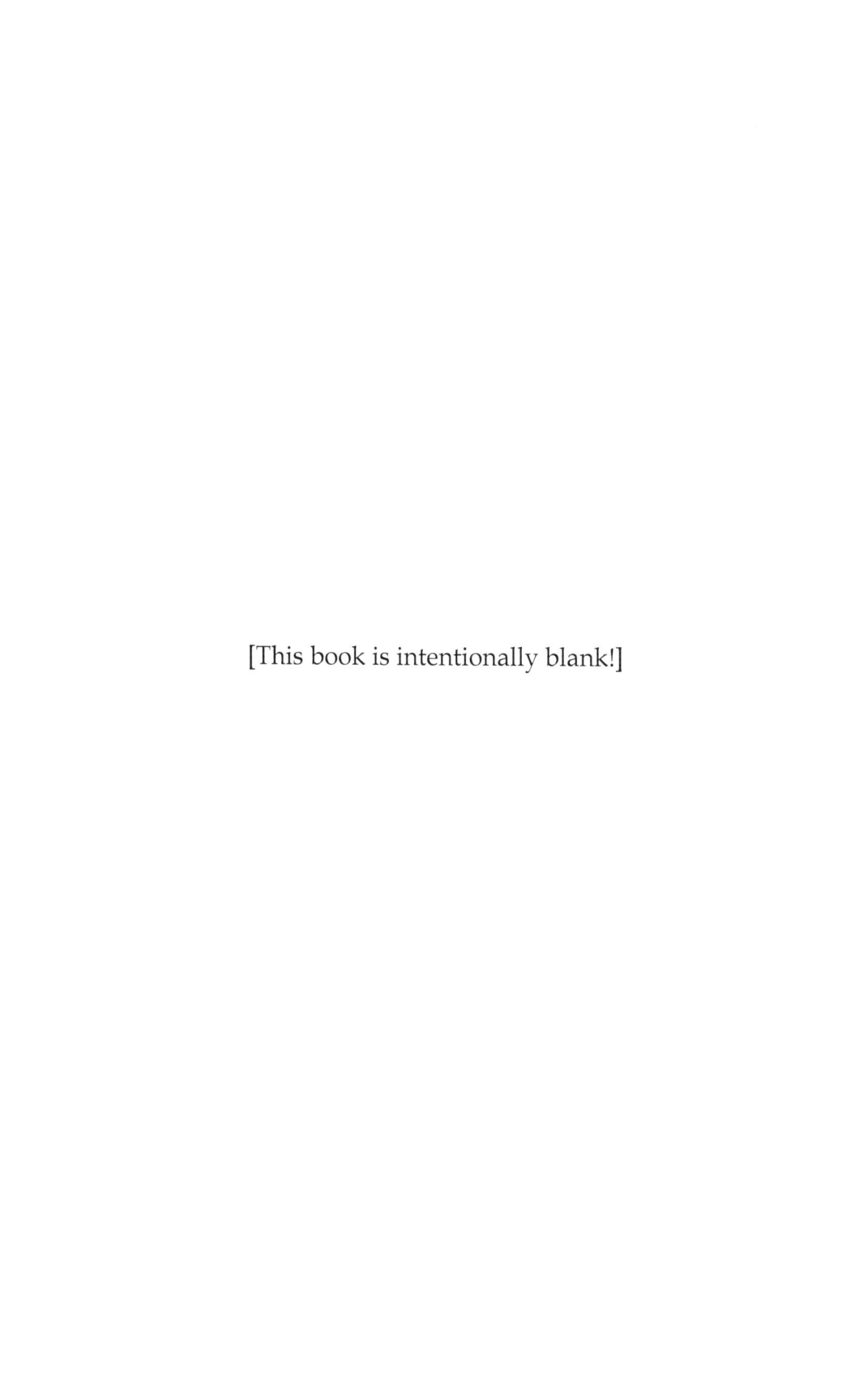

[This book is intentionally blank!]

[This book is intentionally blank!]

[This book is intentionally blank!]

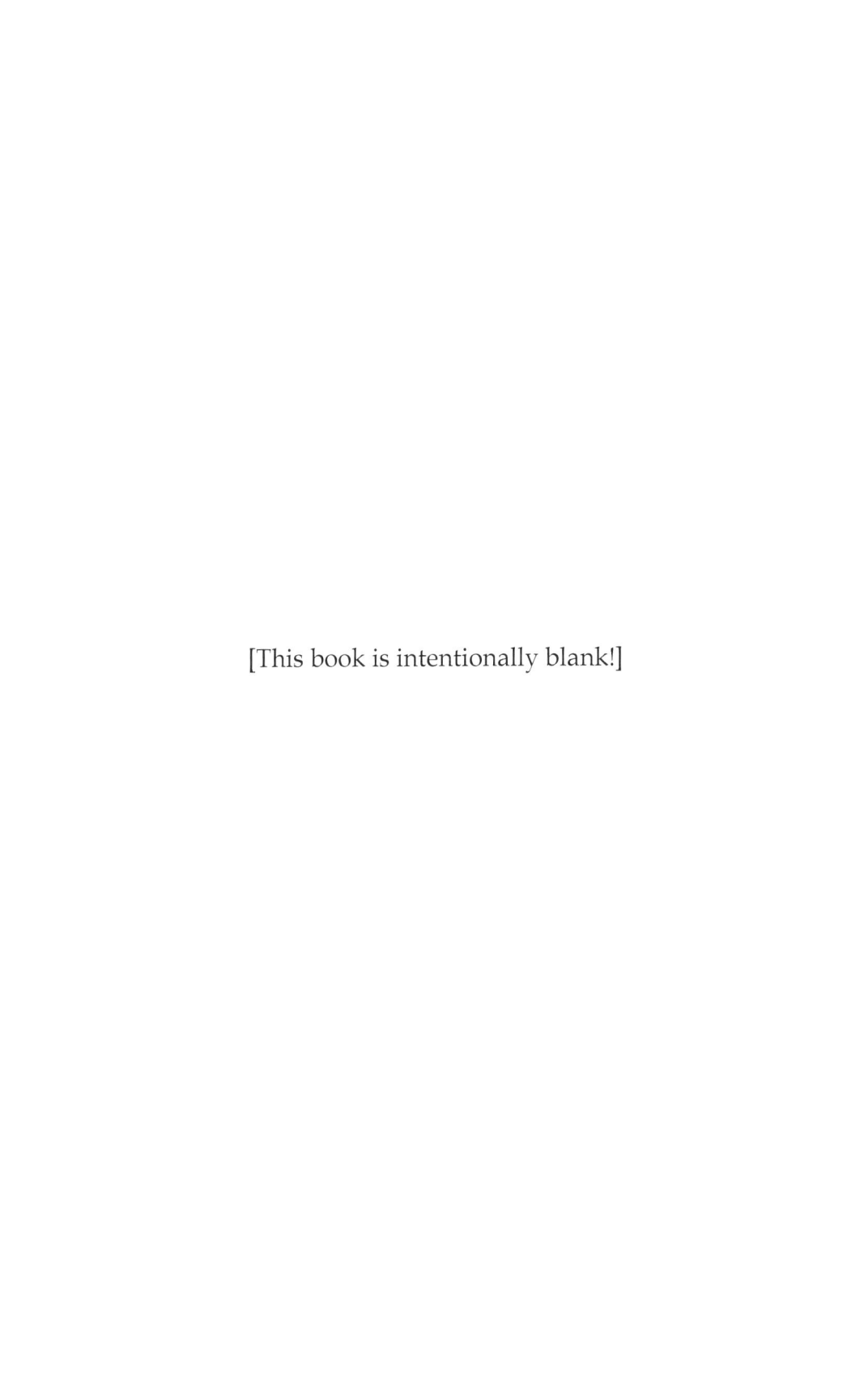

[This book is intentionally blank!]

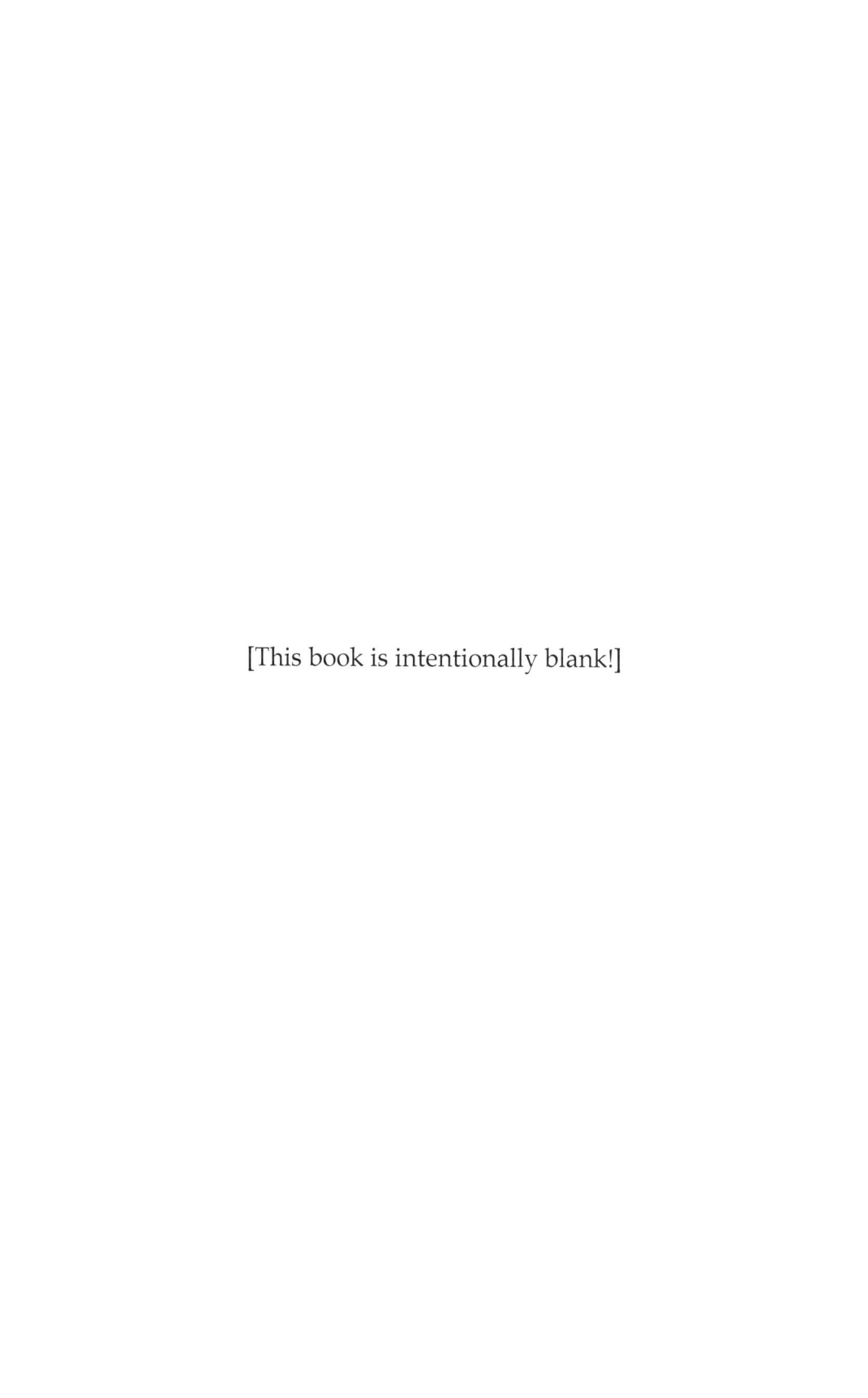

[This book is intentionally blank!]

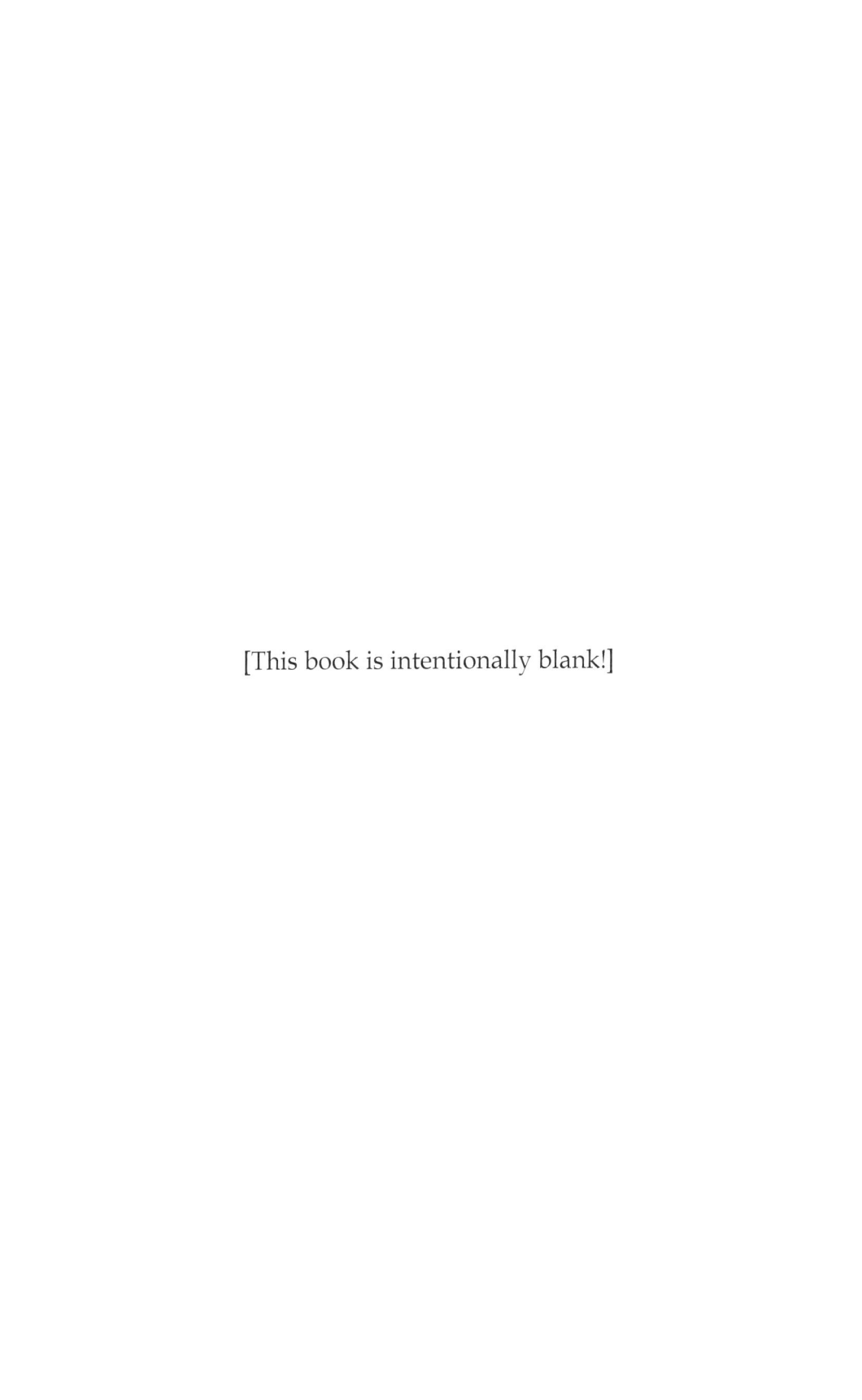

[This book is intentionally blank!]

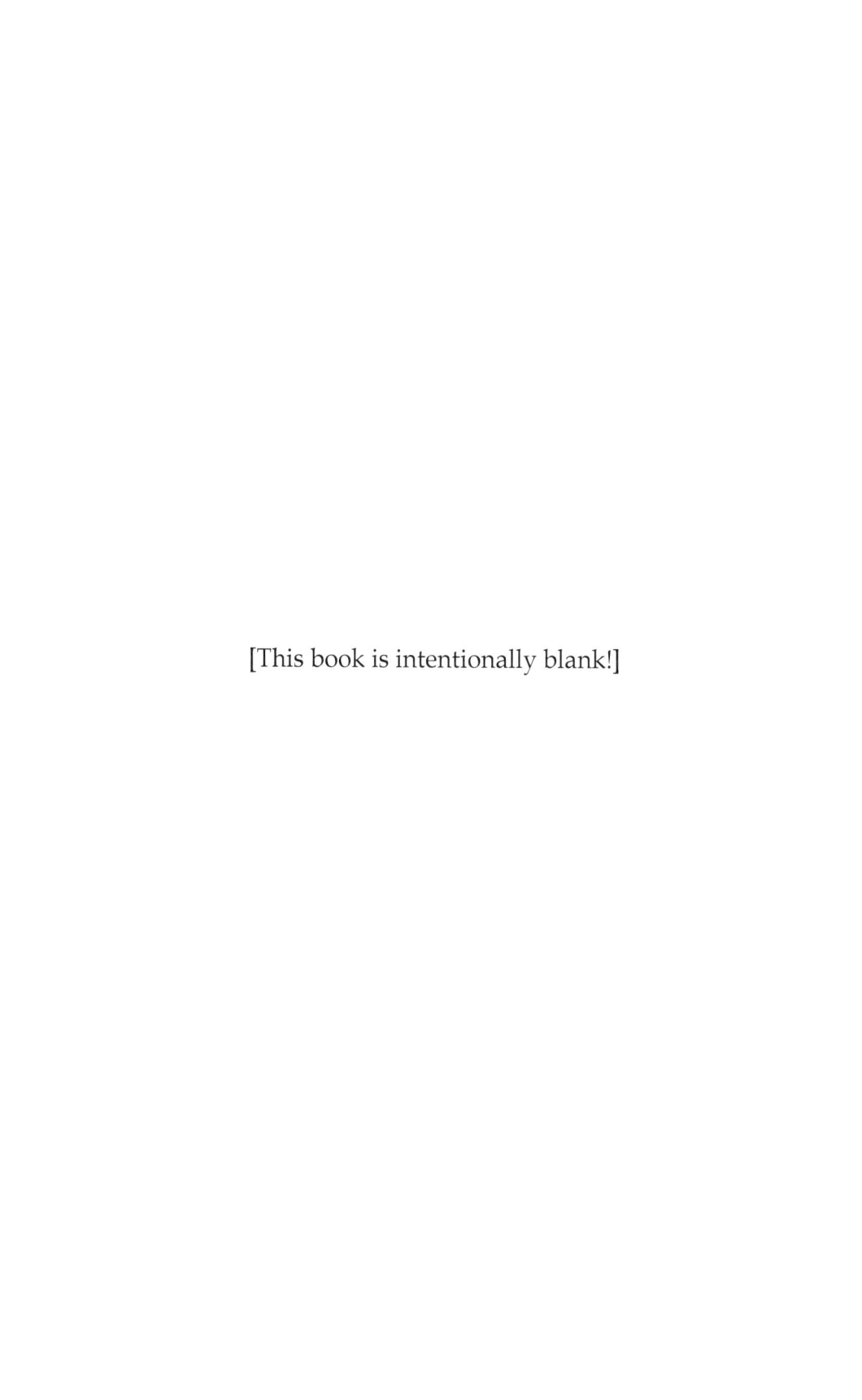

[This book is intentionally blank!]

[This book is intentionally blank!]

[This book is intentionally blank!]

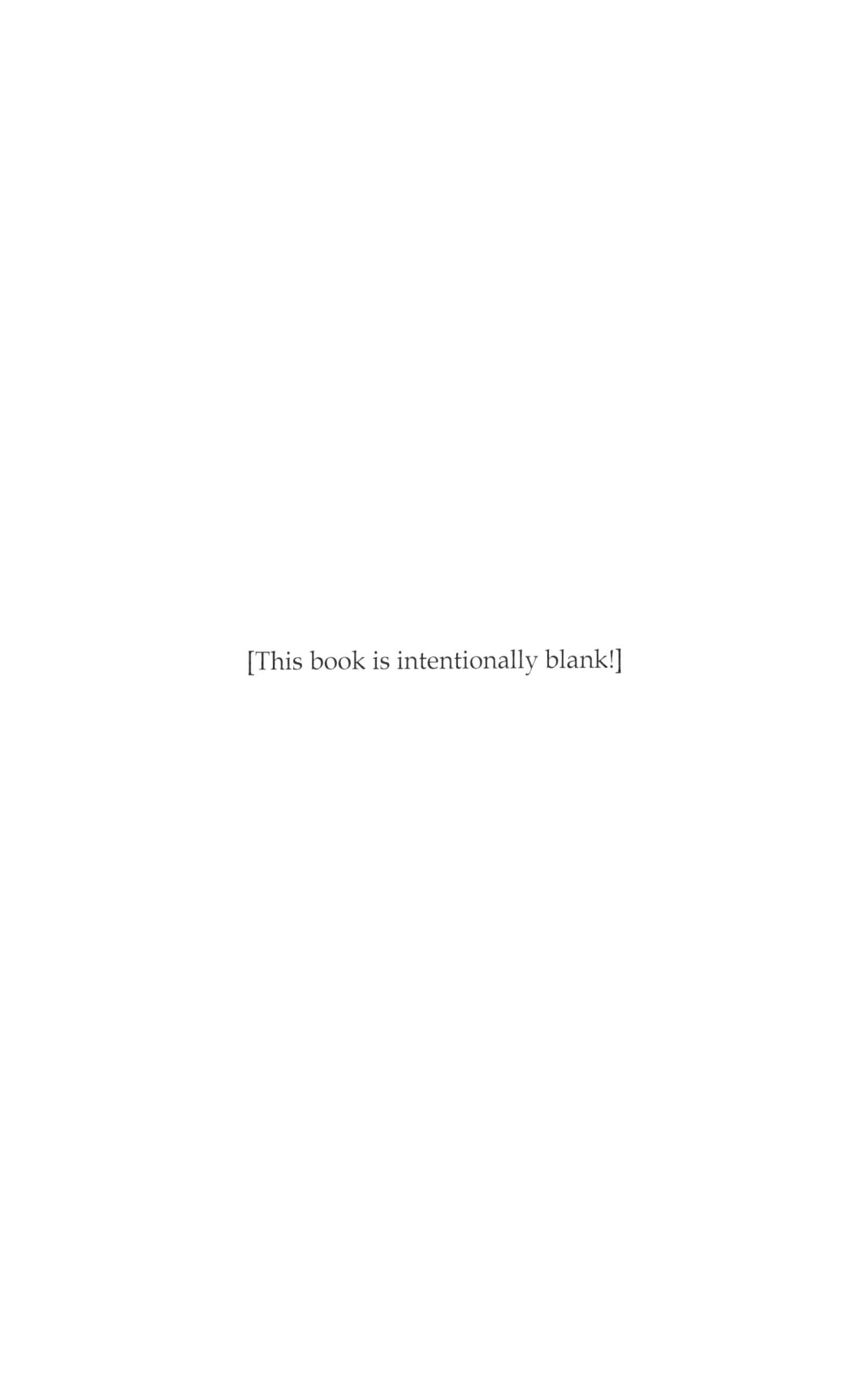

[This book is intentionally blank!]

[This book is intentionally blank!]

[This book is intentionally blank!]

[This book is intentionally blank!]

[This book is intentionally blank!]

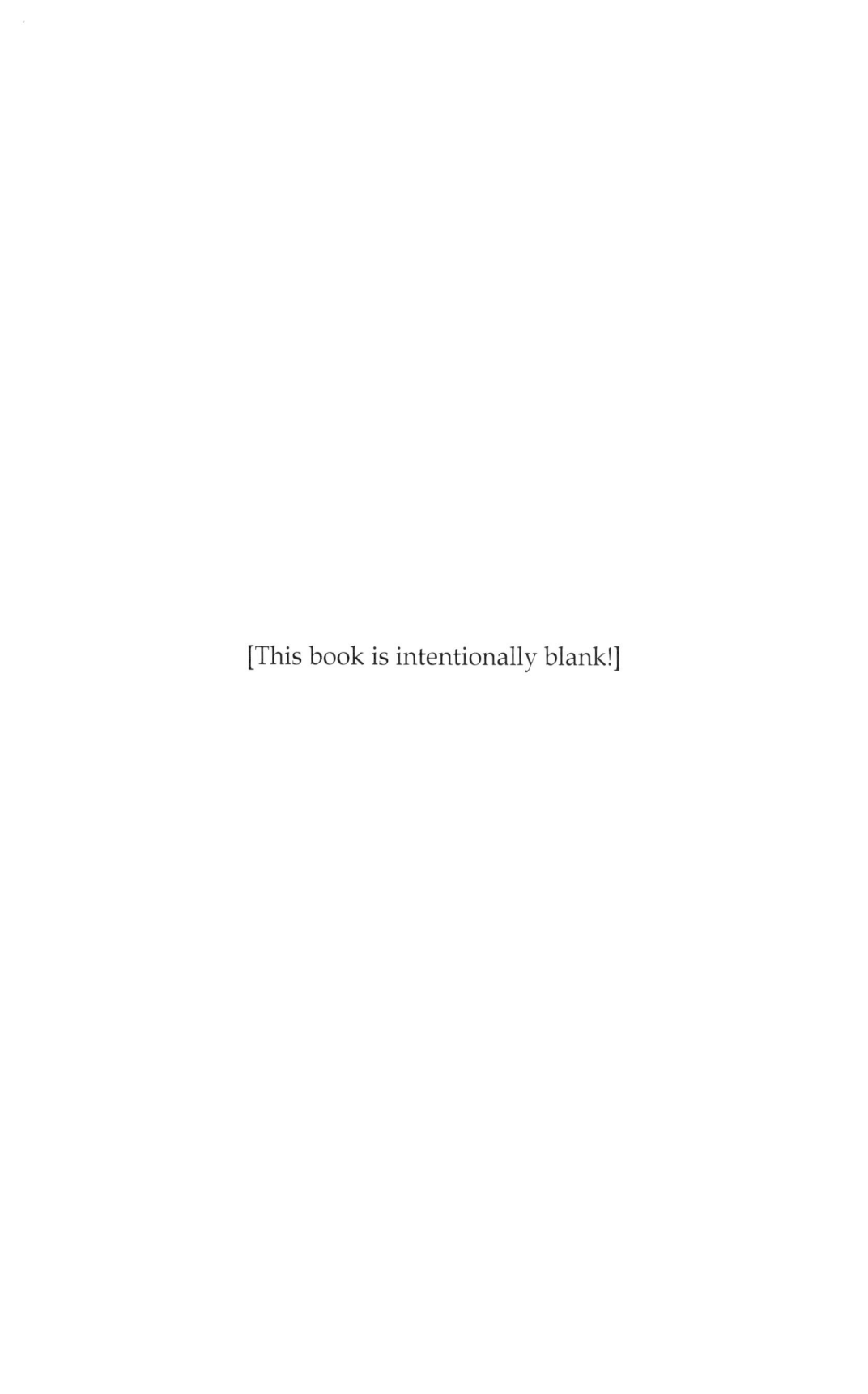

[This book is intentionally blank!]

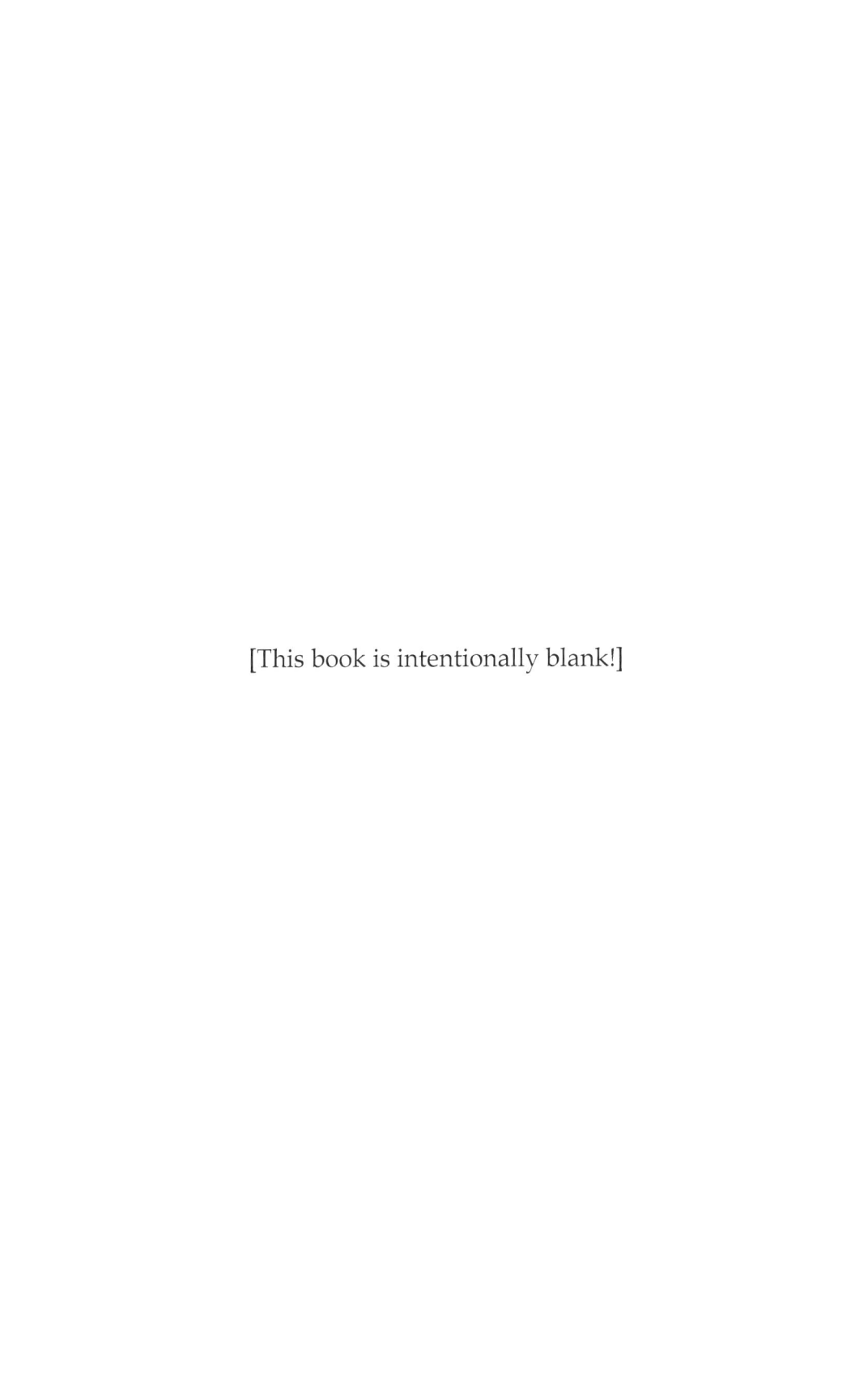

[This book is intentionally blank!]

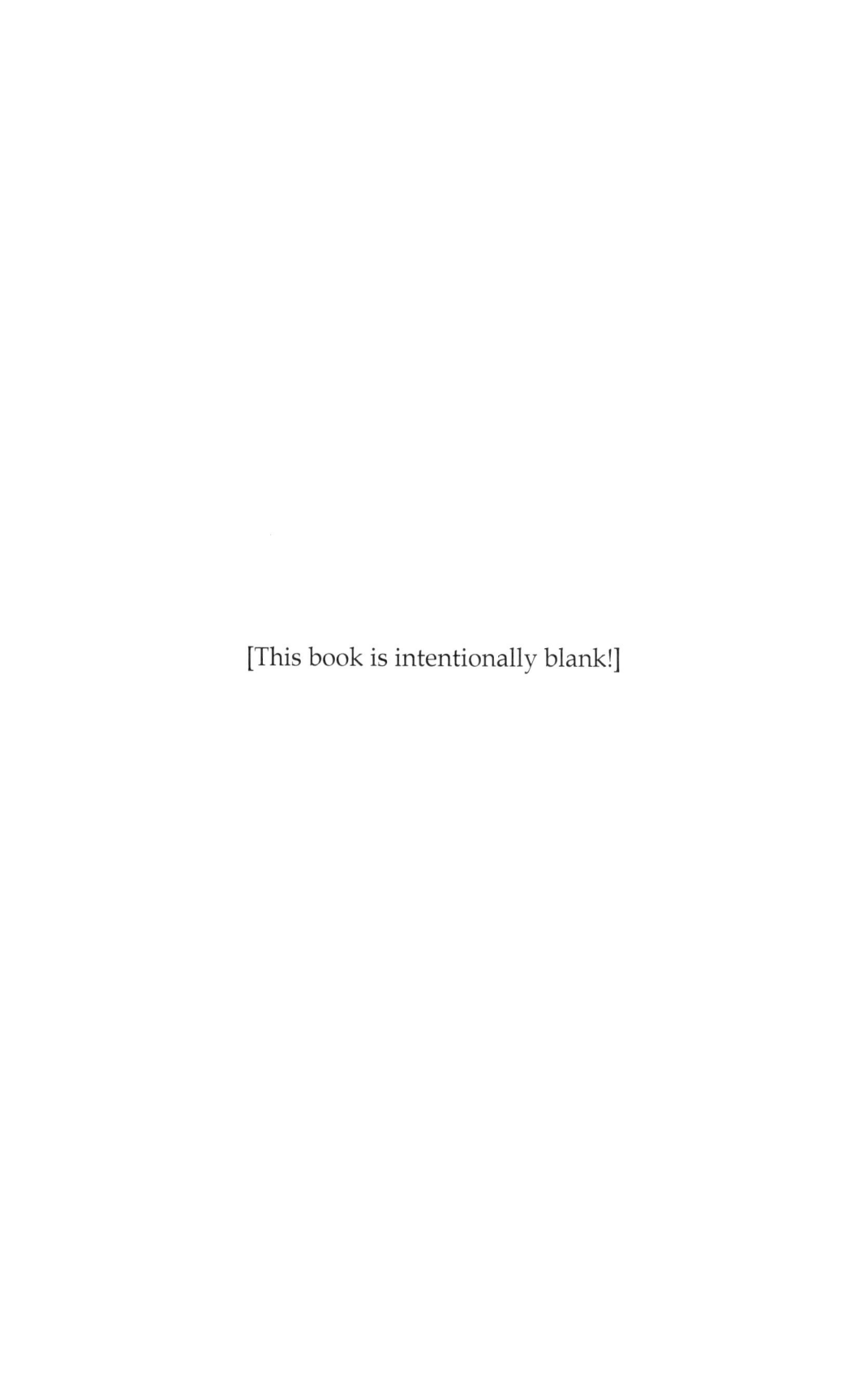

[This book is intentionally blank!]

[This book is intentionally blank!]

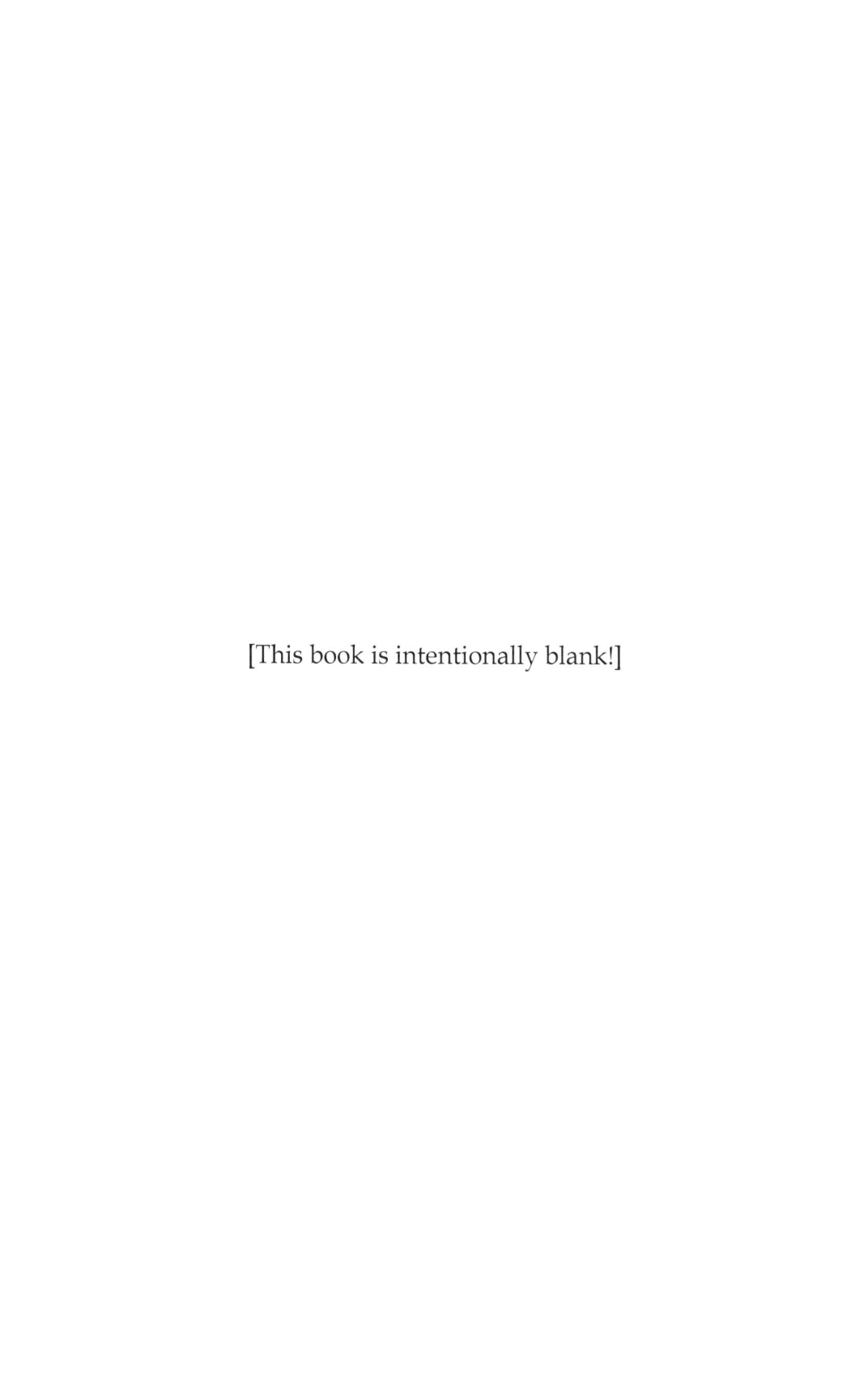

[This book is intentionally blank!]

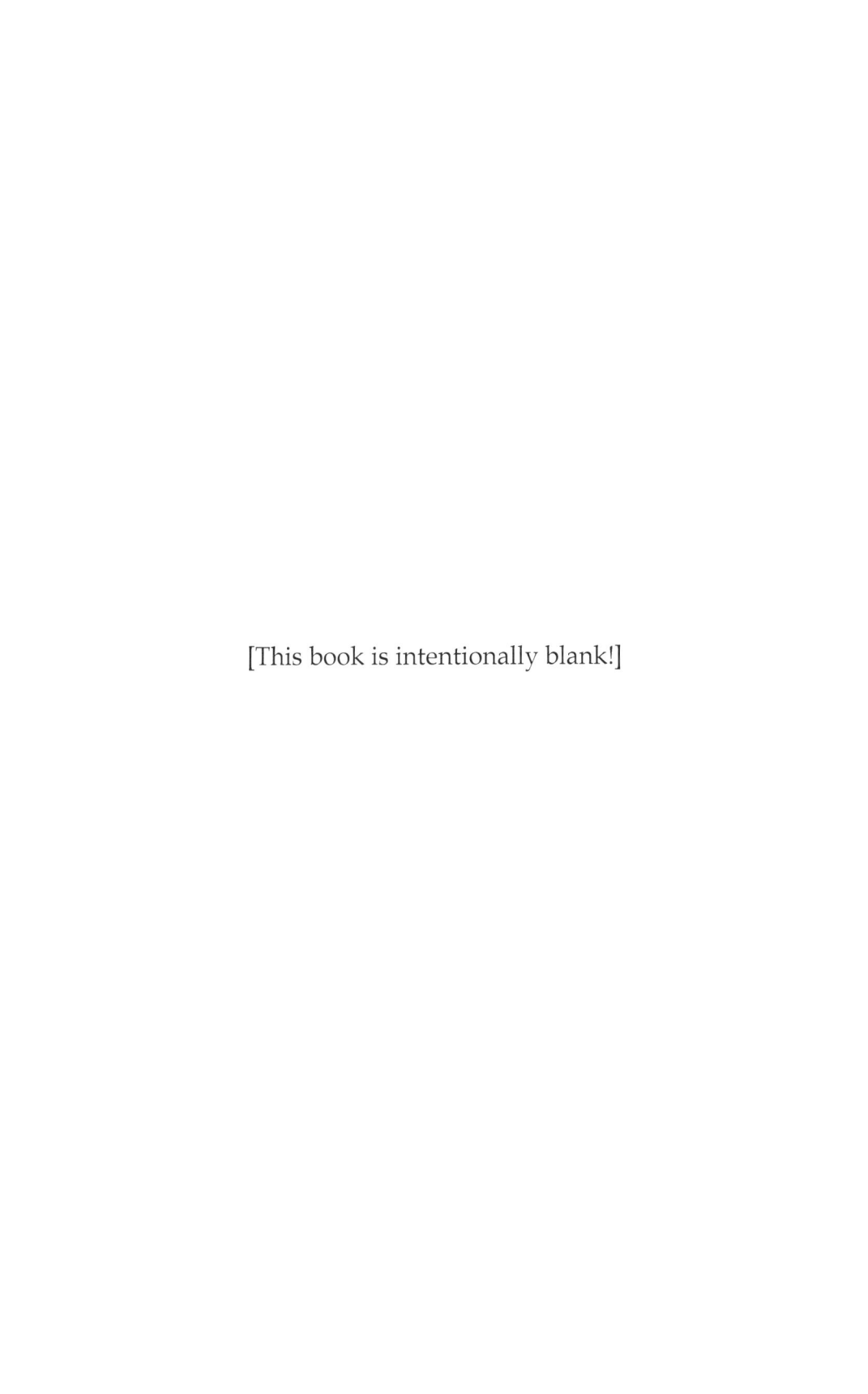

[This book is intentionally blank!]

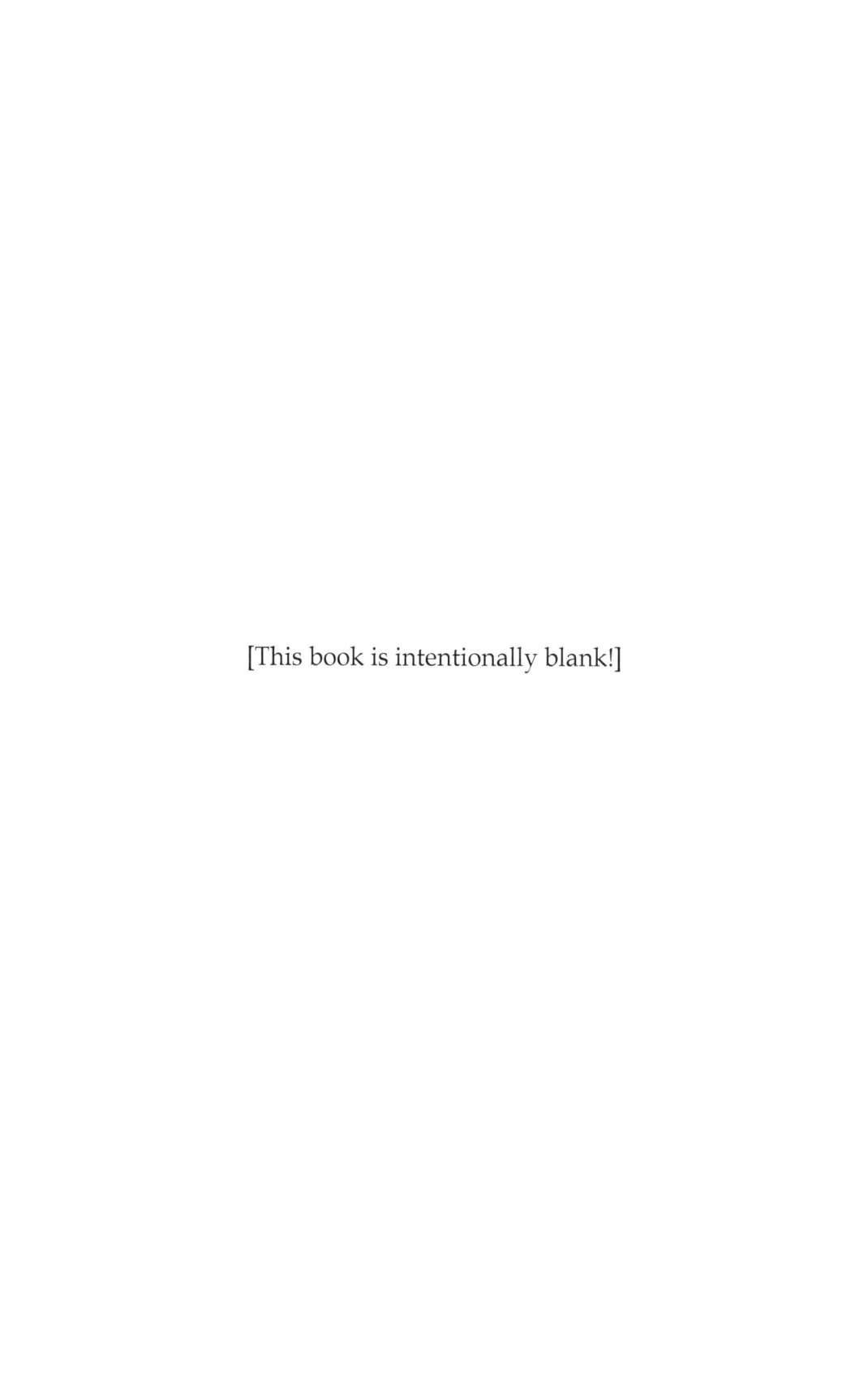

[This book is intentionally blank!]

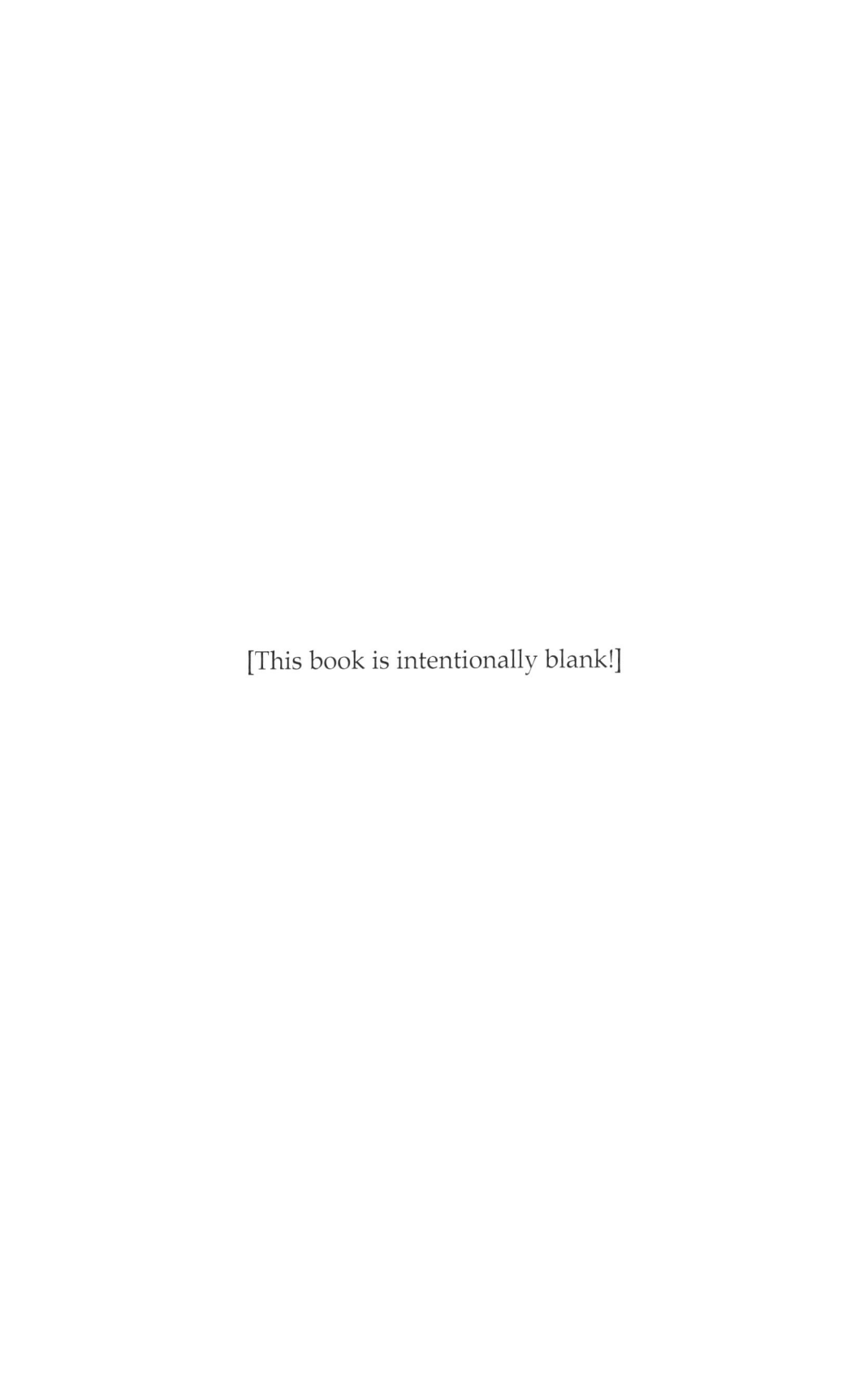

[This book is intentionally blank!]

[This book is intentionally blank!]

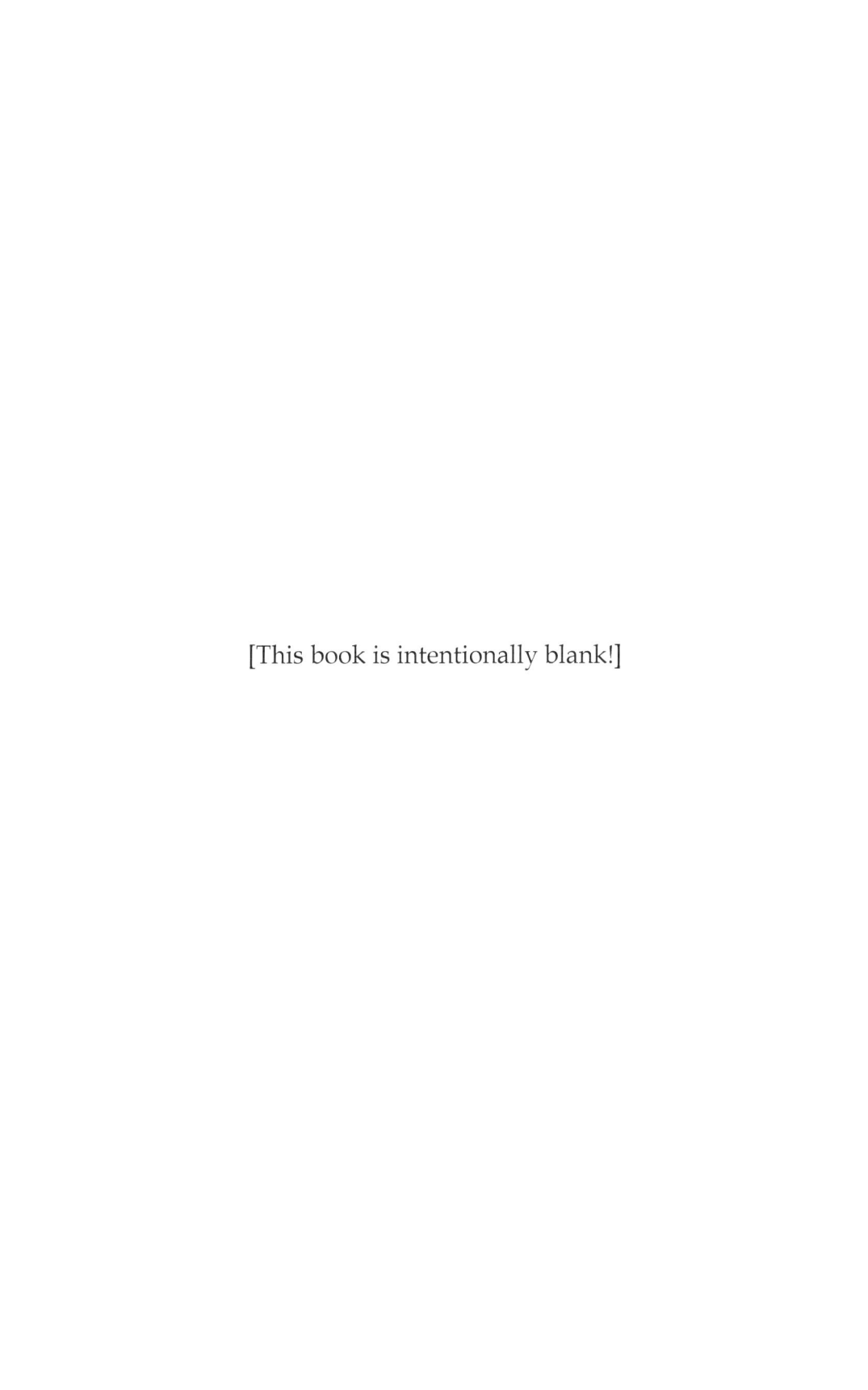

[This book is intentionally blank!]

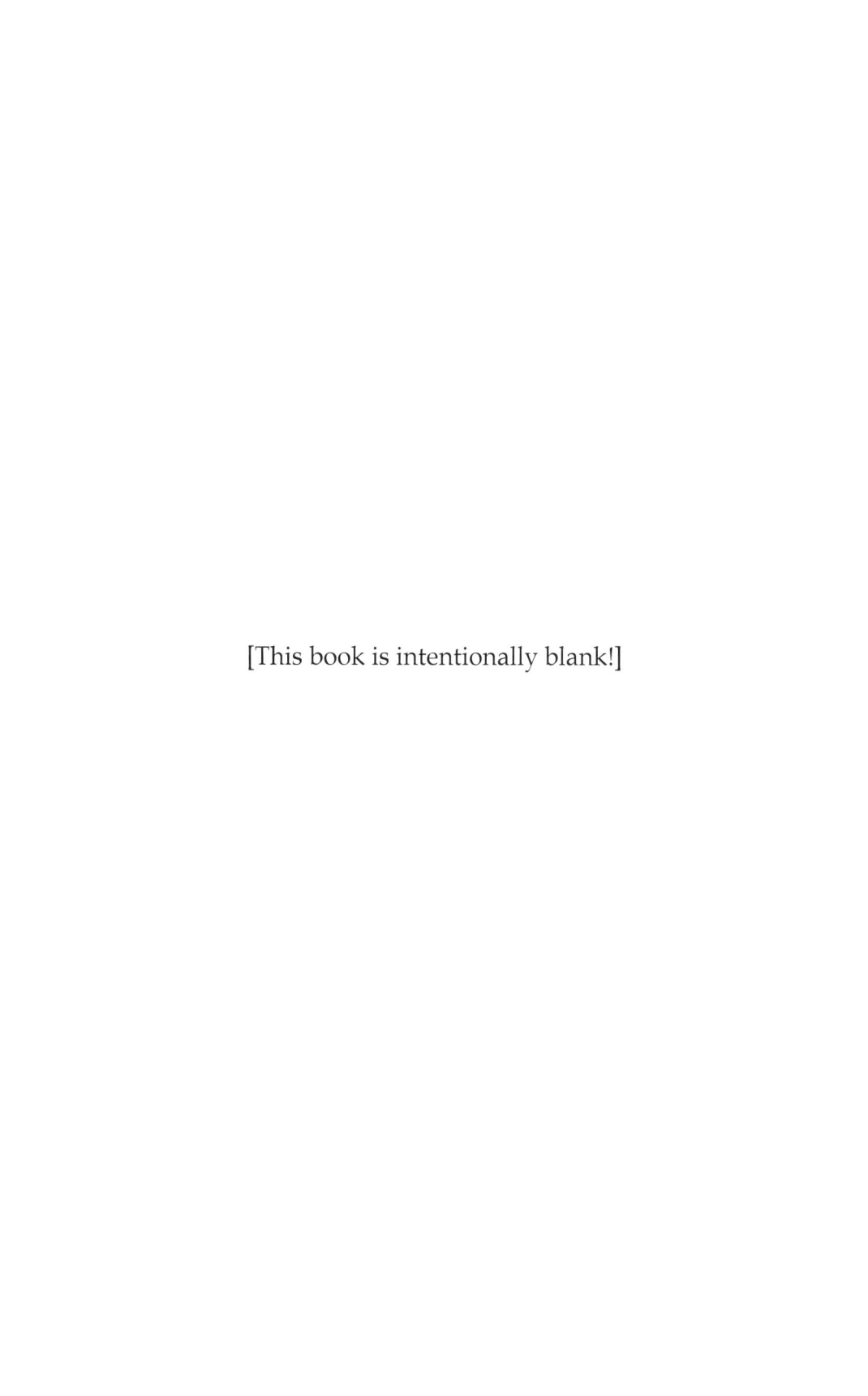

[This book is intentionally blank!]

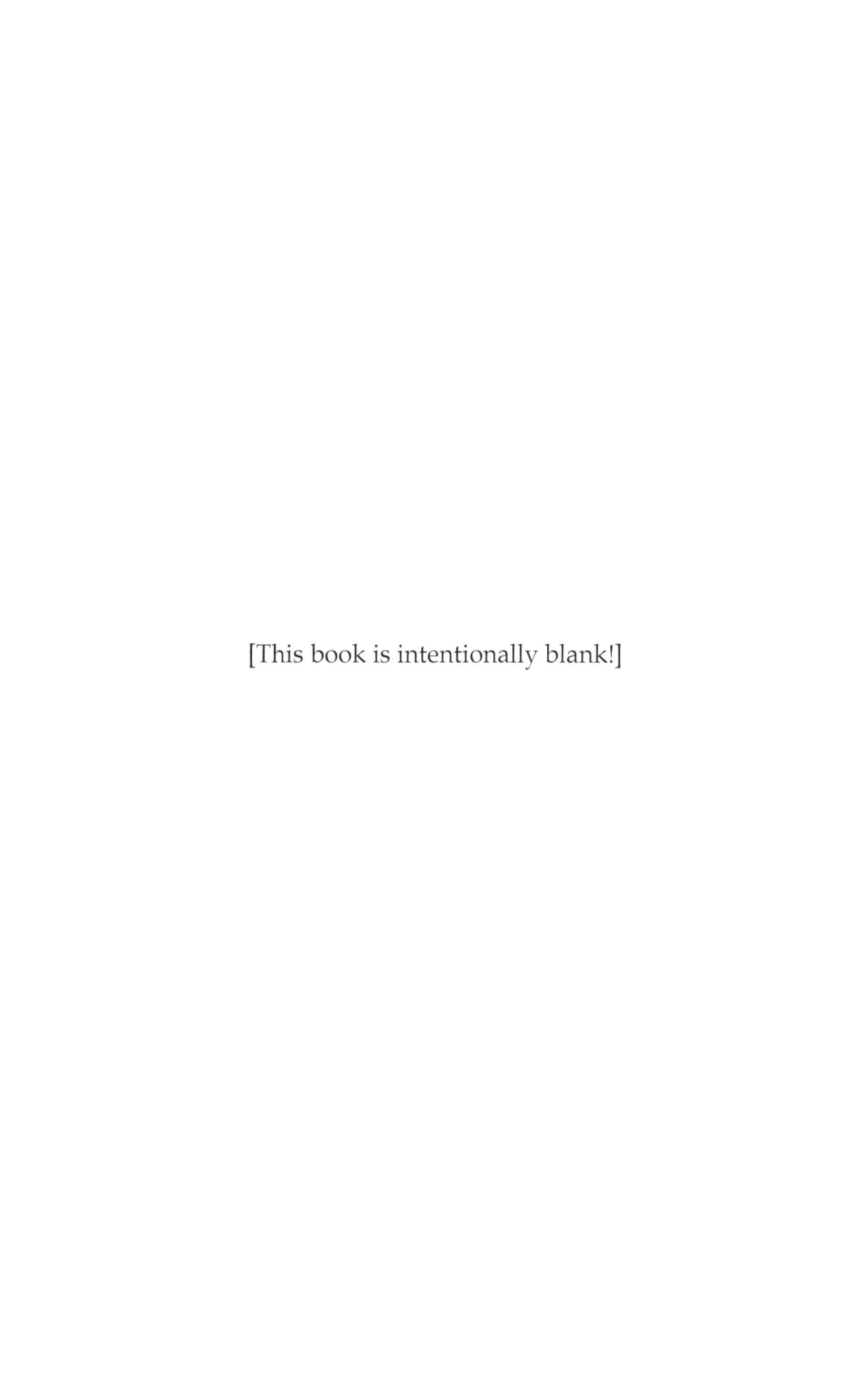

[This book is intentionally blank!]

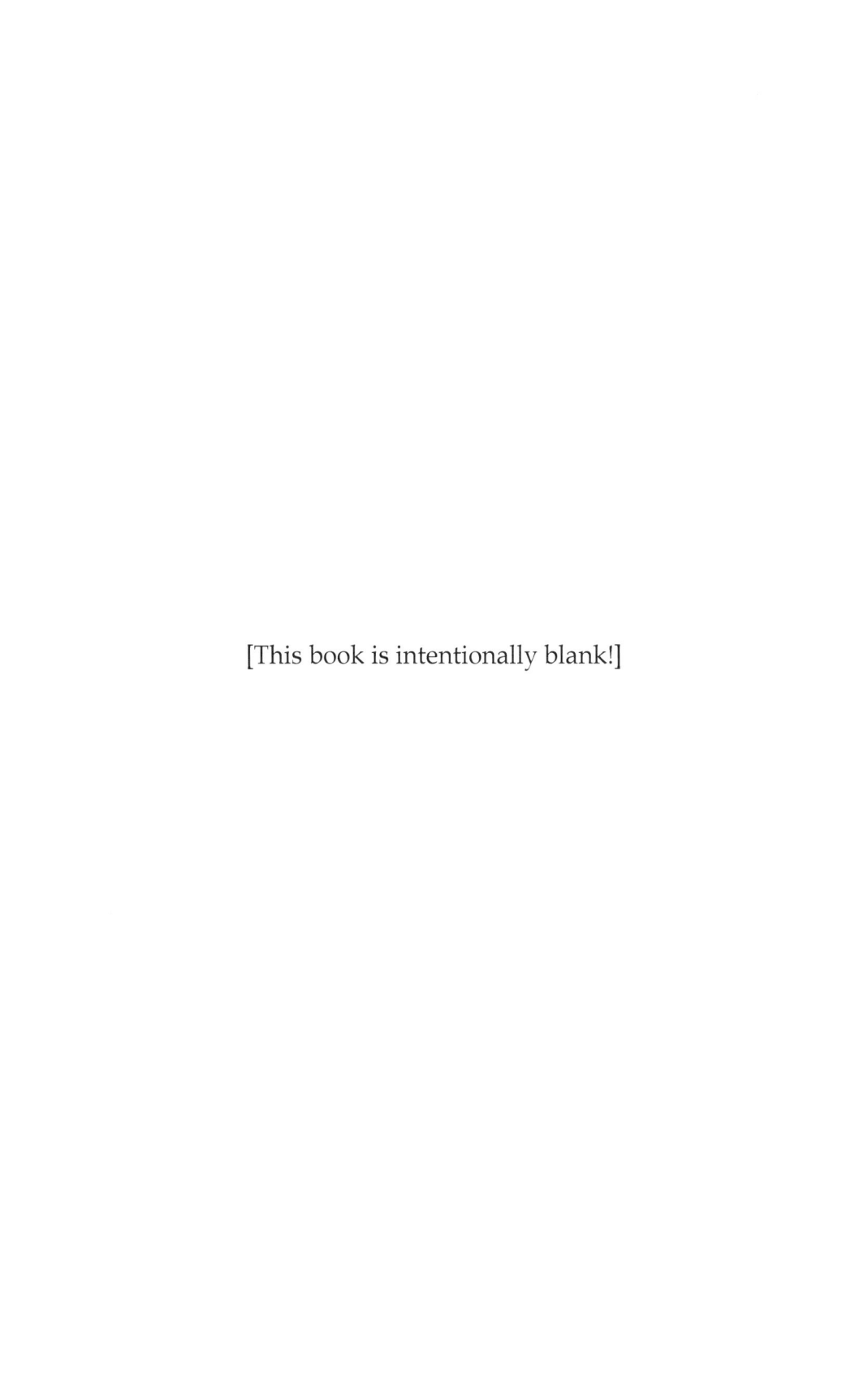

[This book is intentionally blank!]

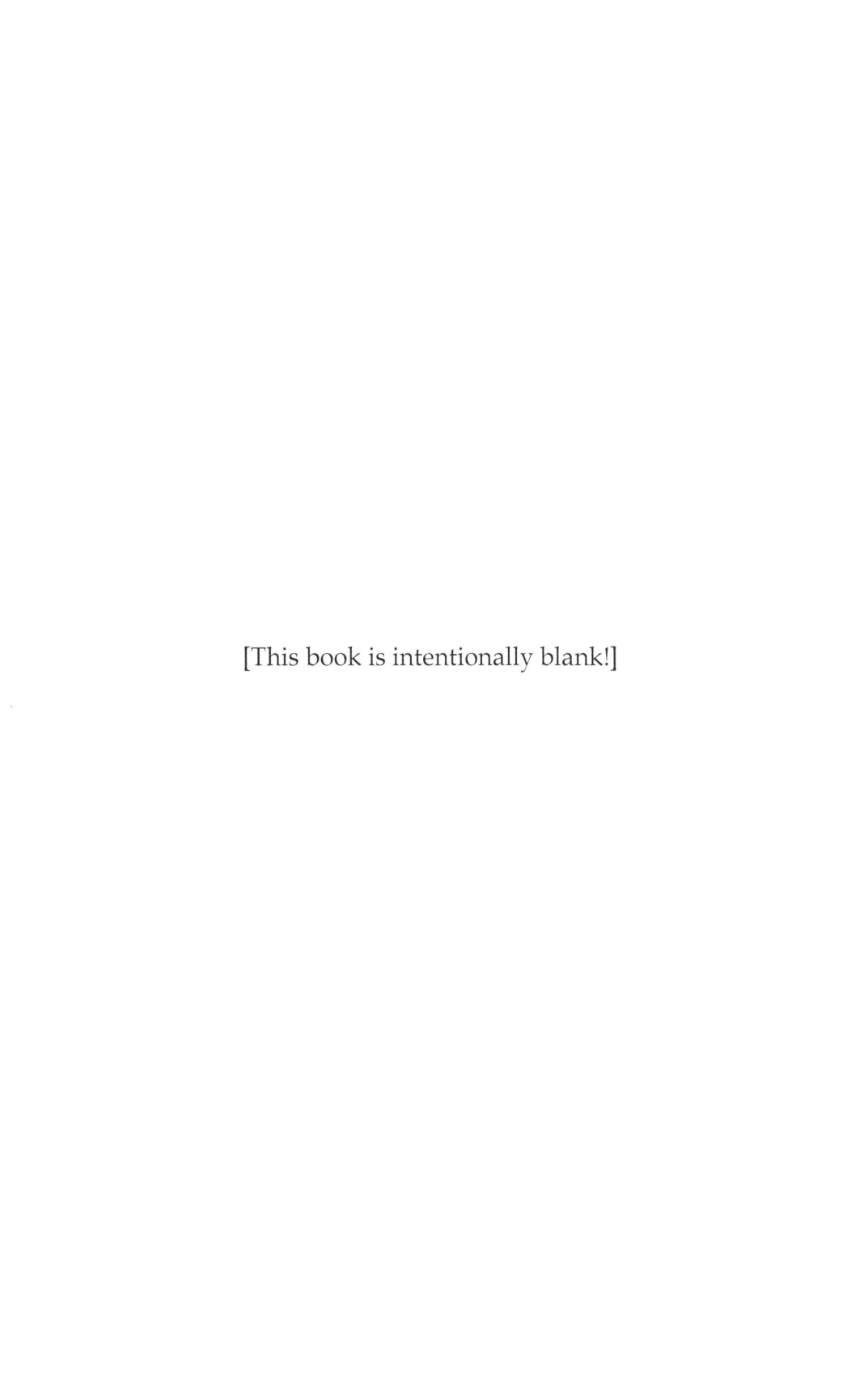

[This book is intentionally blank!]

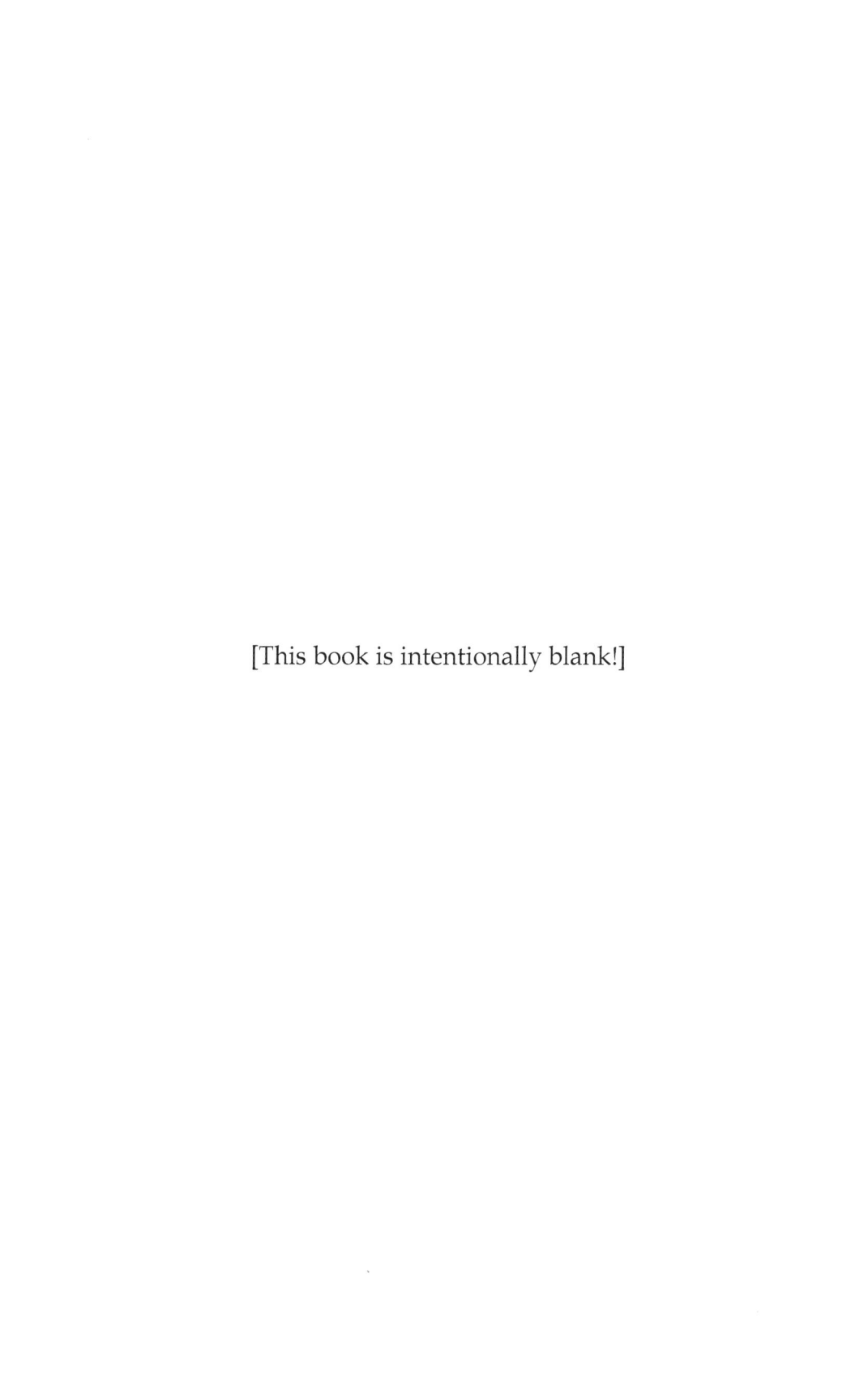

[This book is intentionally blank!]

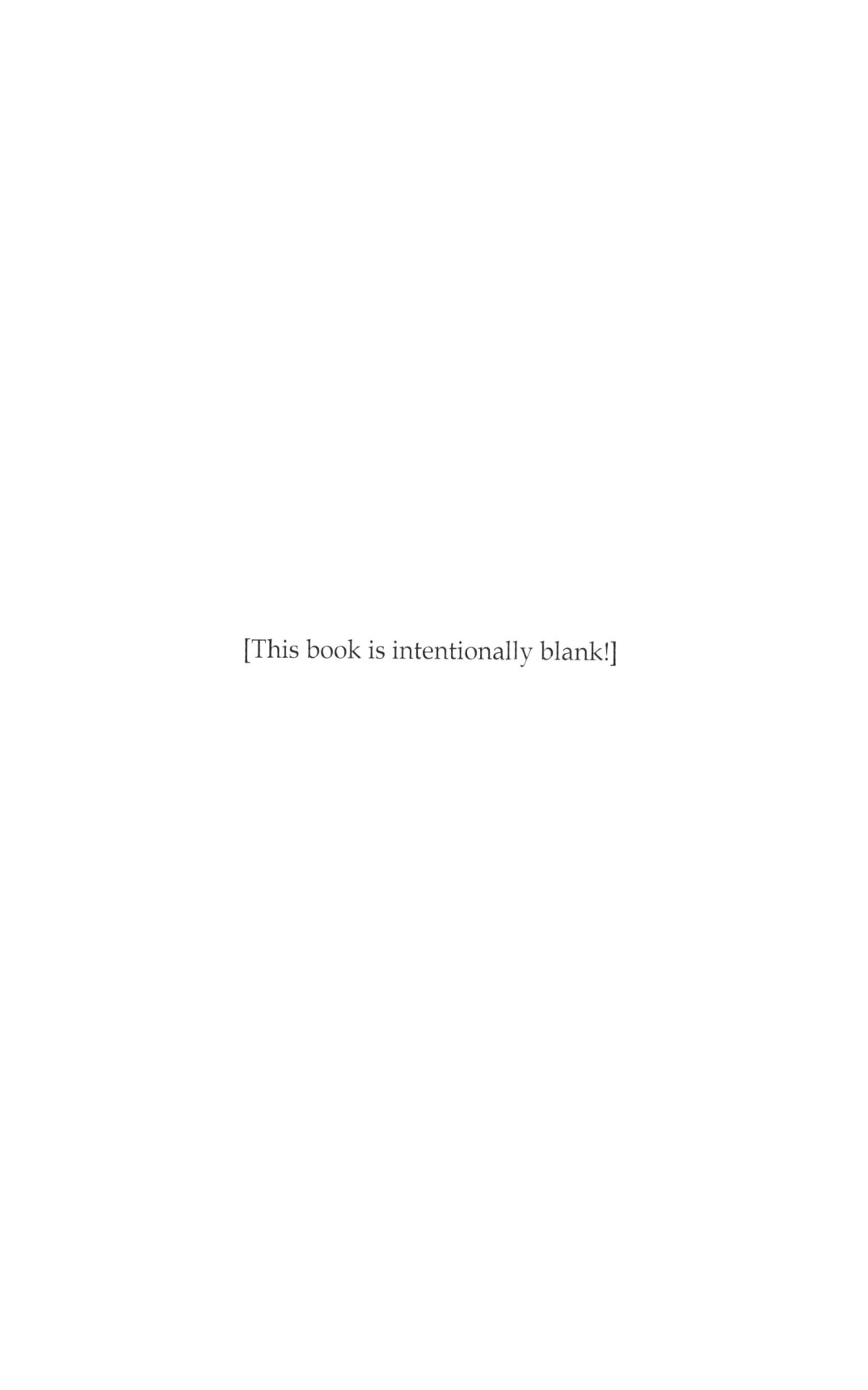

[This book is intentionally blank!]

[This book is intentionally blank!]

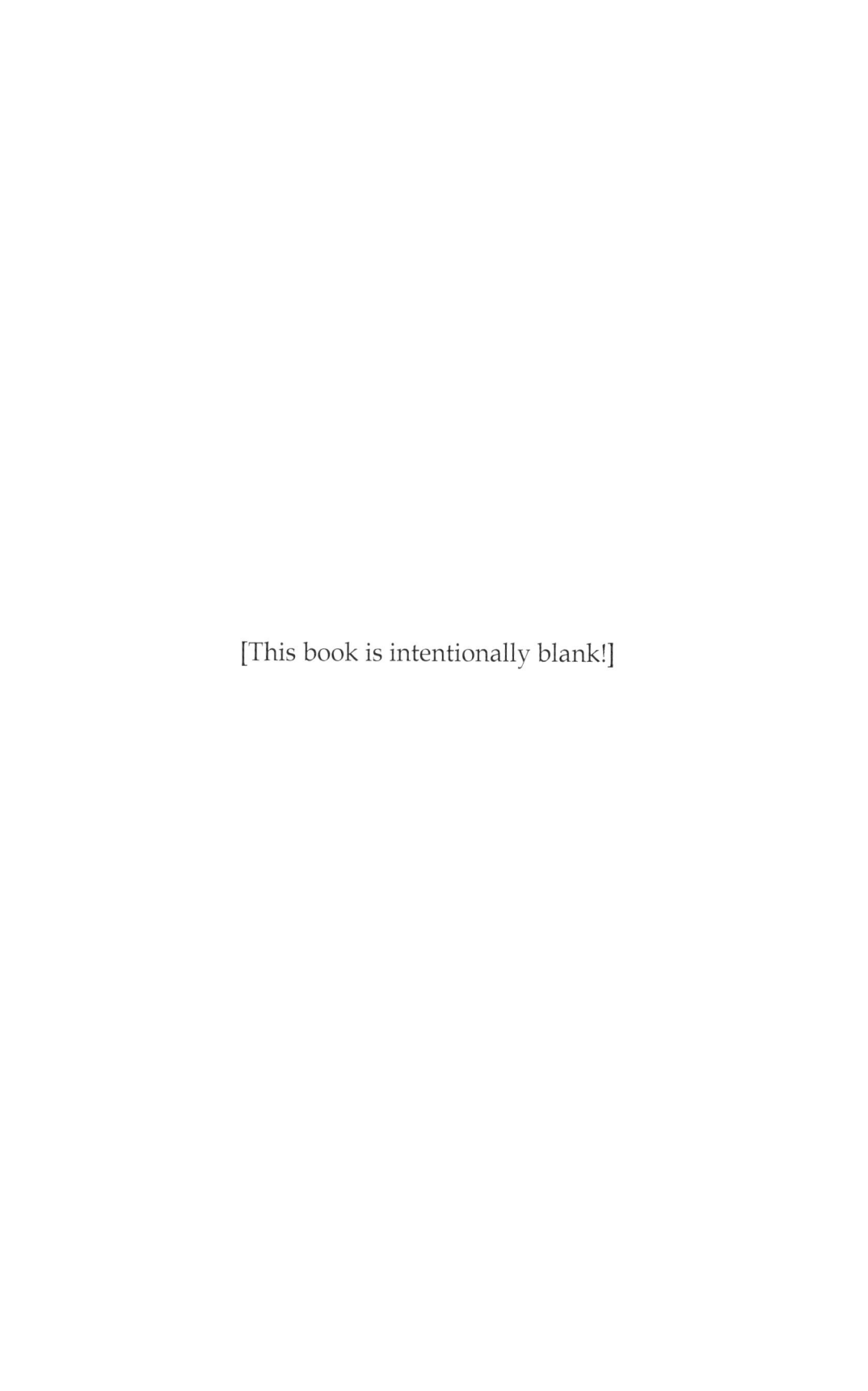

[This book is intentionally blank!]

[This book is intentionally blank!]

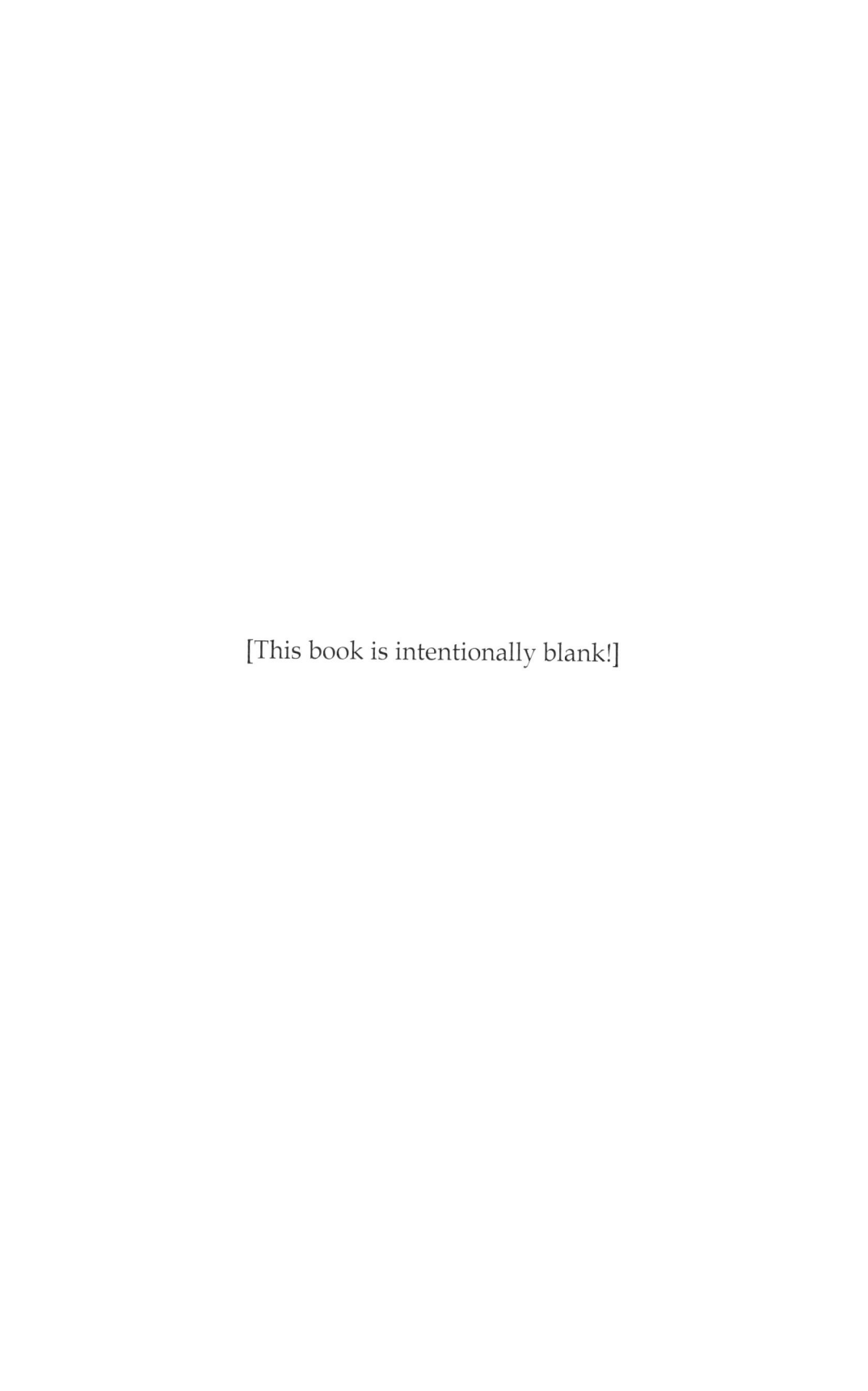

[This book is intentionally blank!]

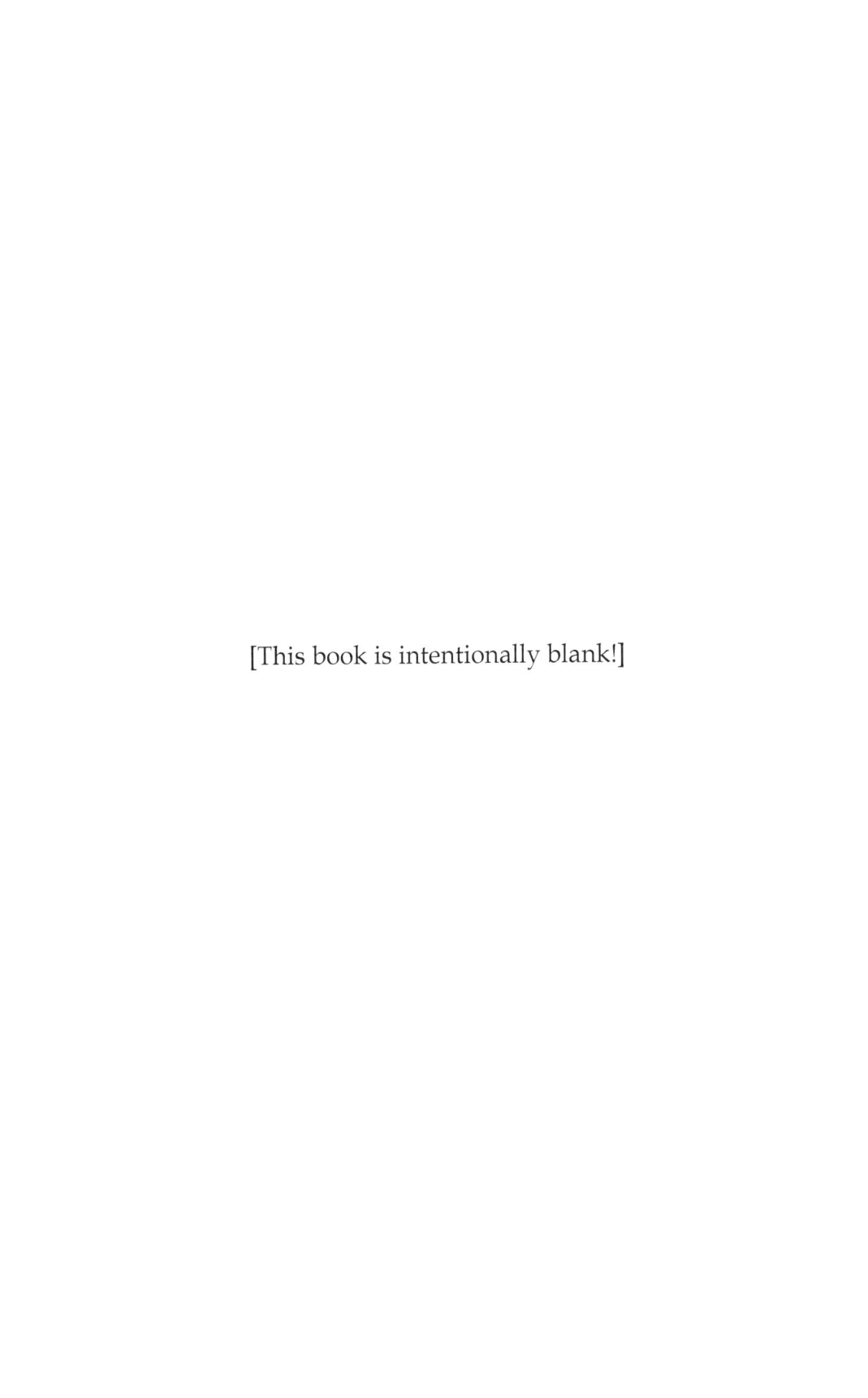

[This book is intentionally blank!]

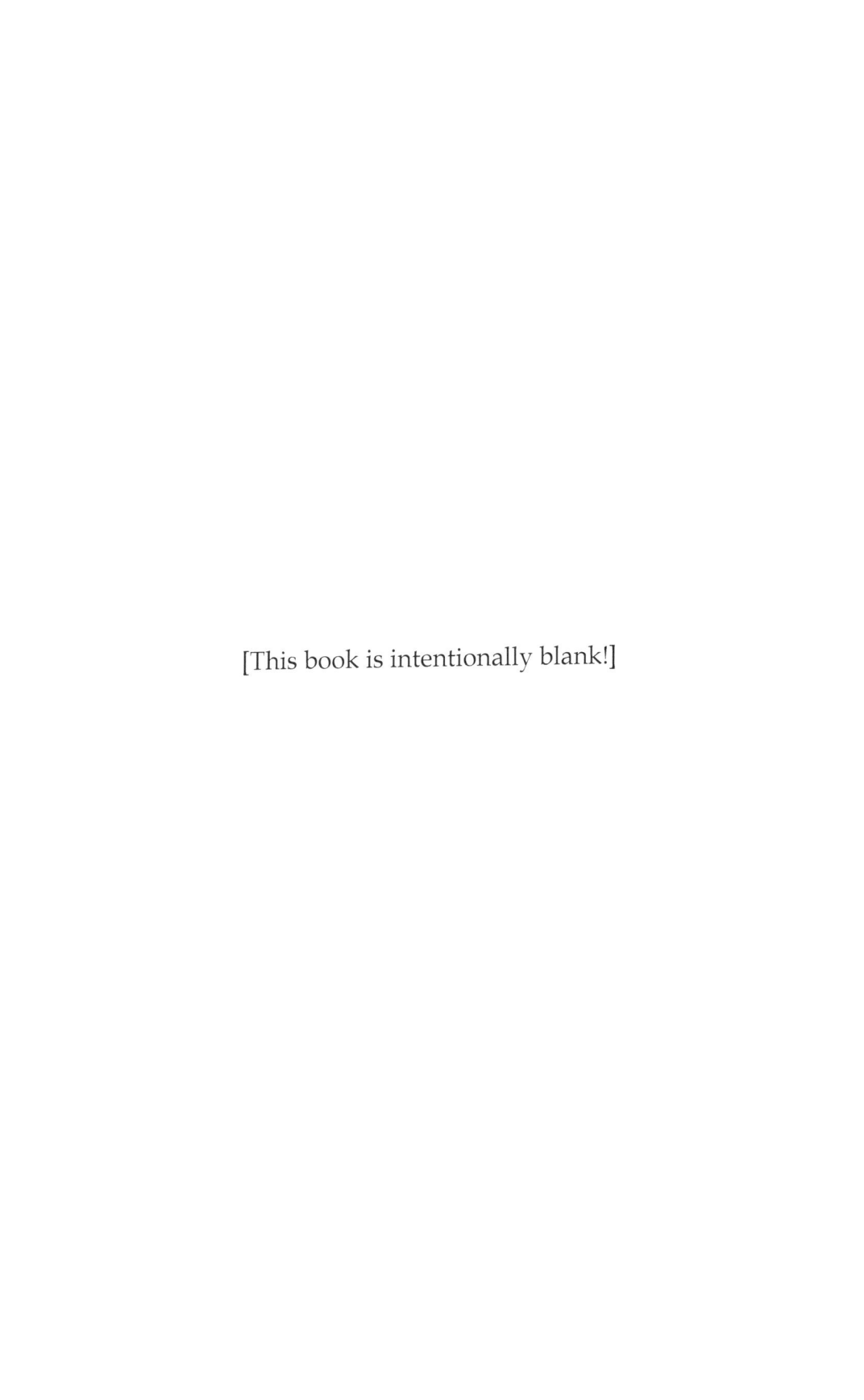

[This book is intentionally blank!]

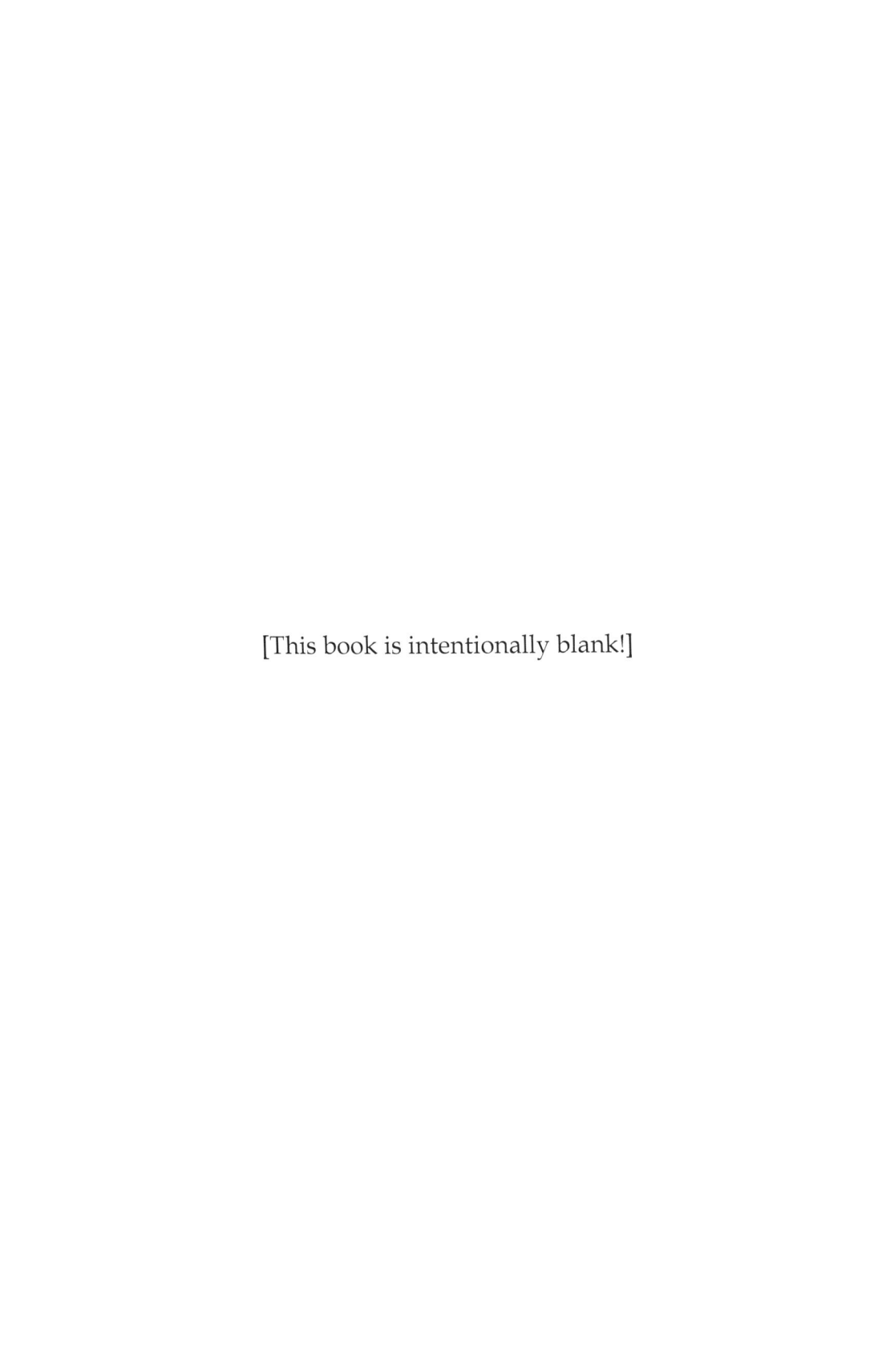

[This book is intentionally blank!]

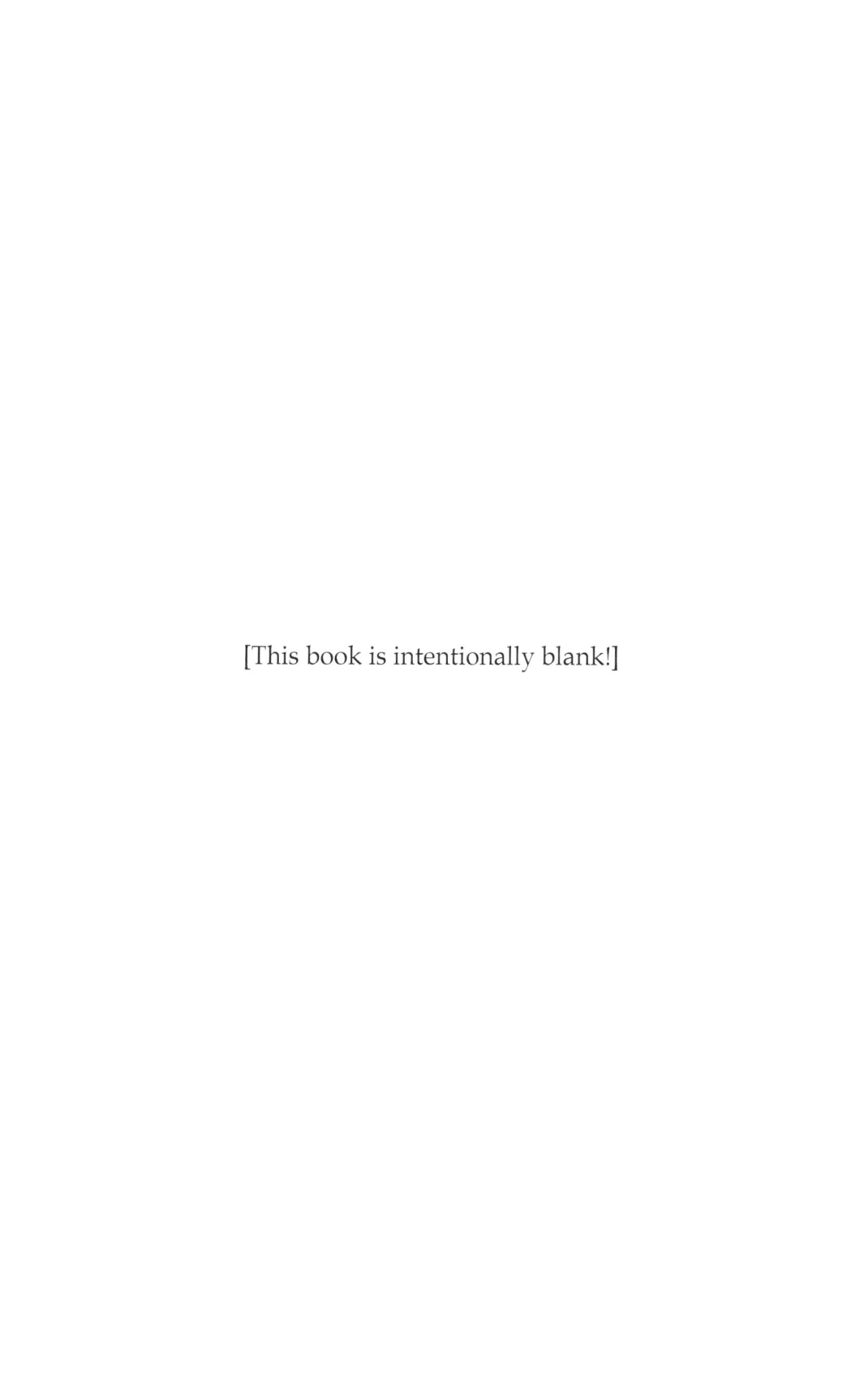

[This book is intentionally blank!]

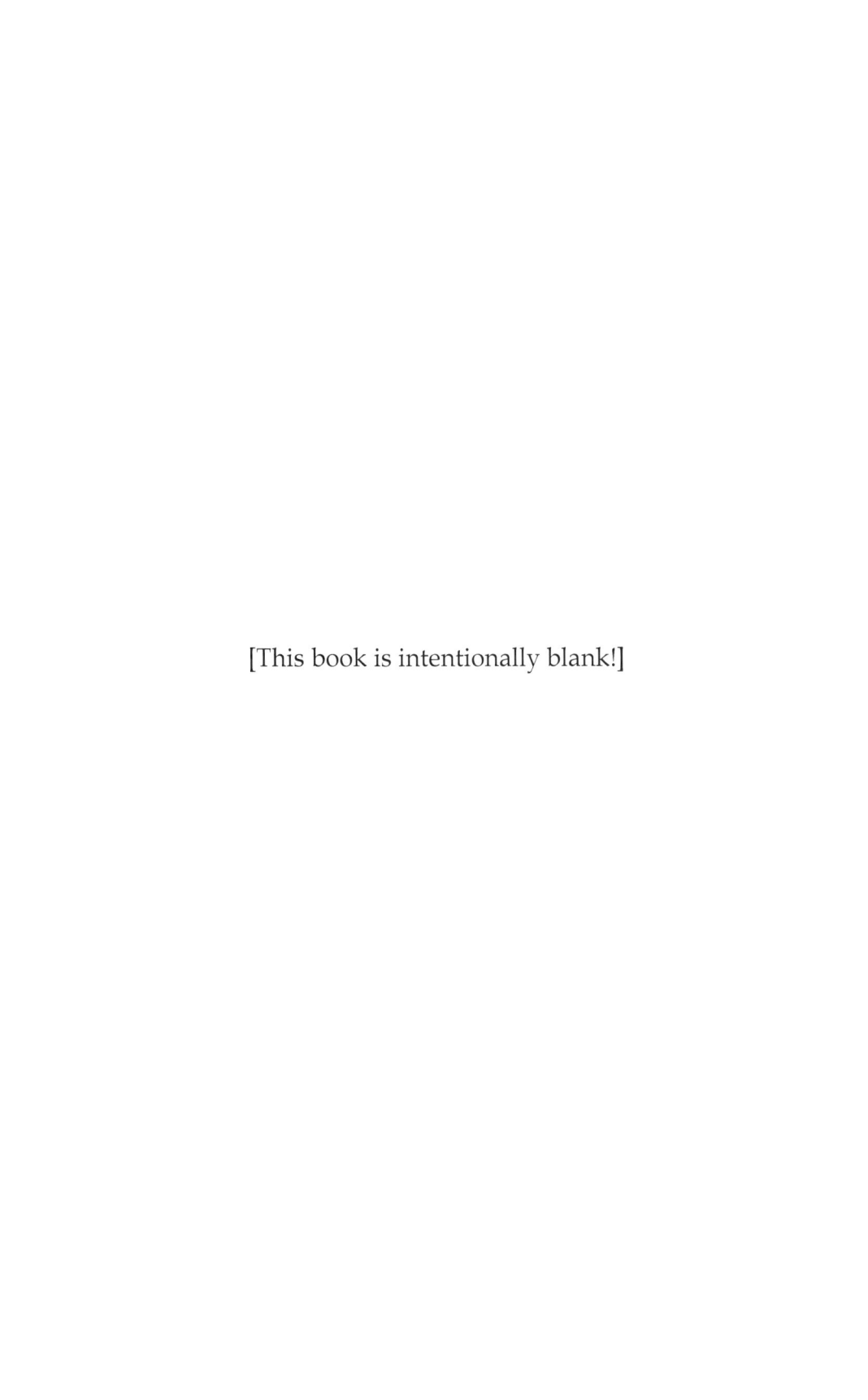

[This book is intentionally blank!]

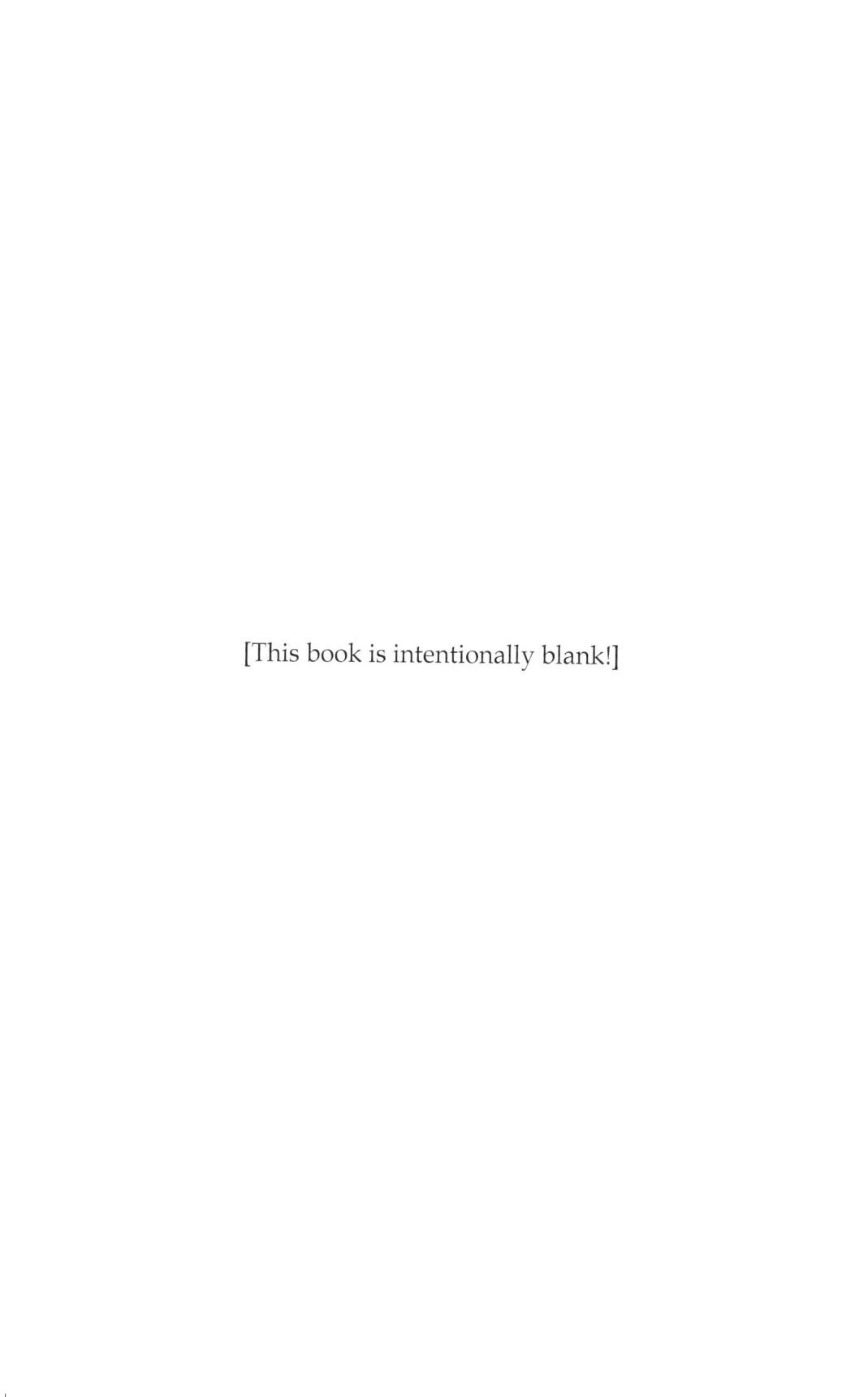

[This book is intentionally blank!]

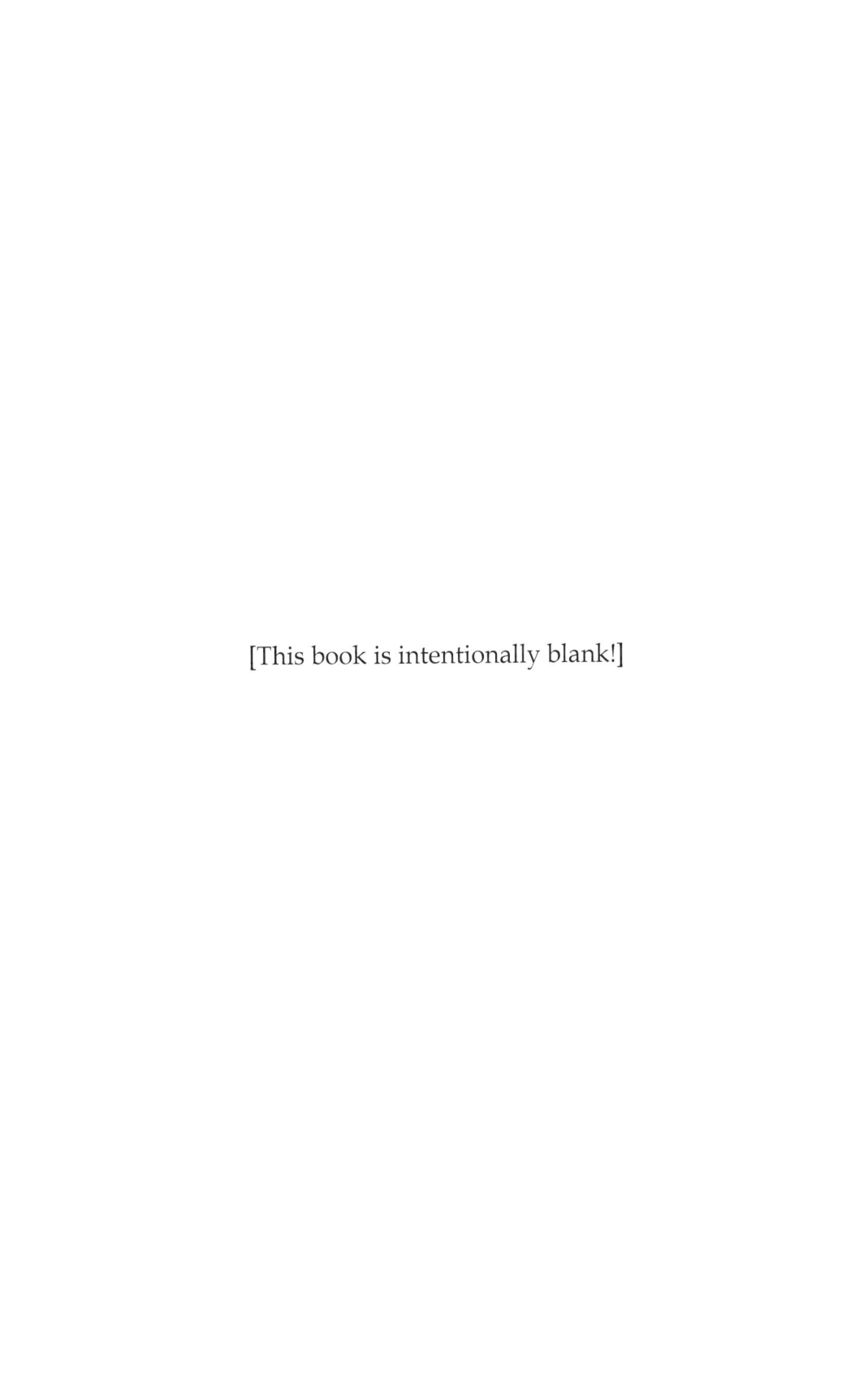

[This book is intentionally blank!]

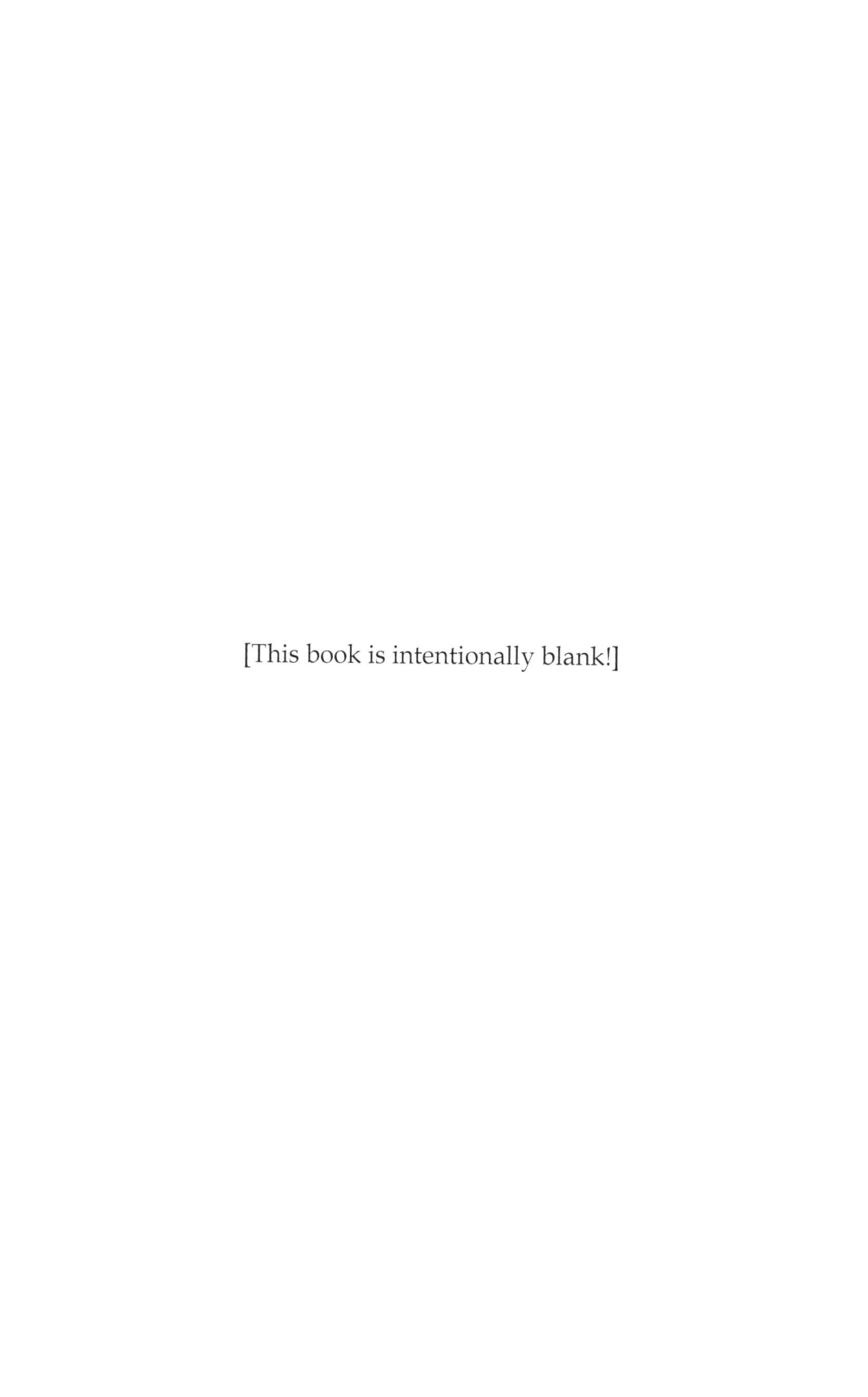

[This book is intentionally blank!]

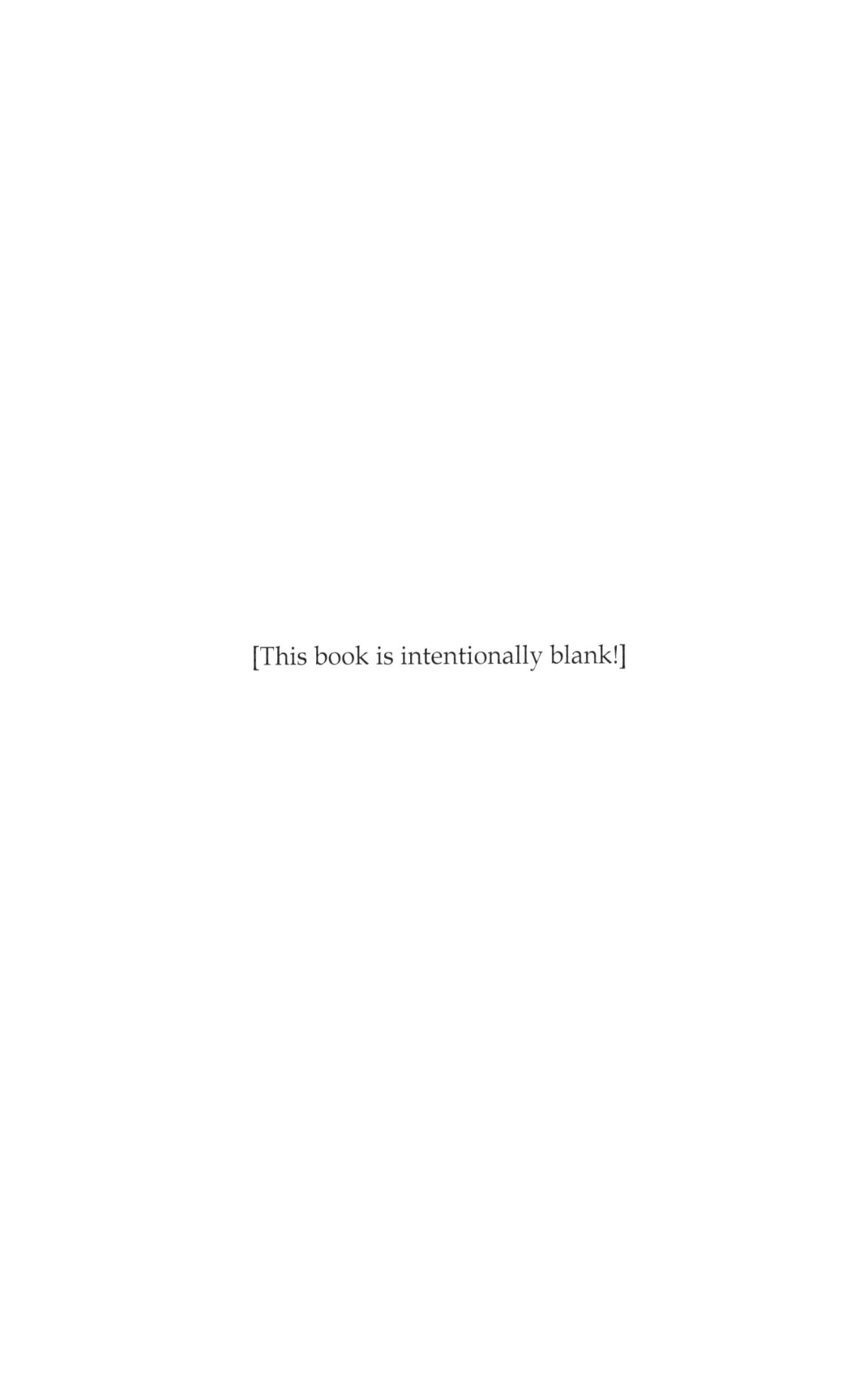

[This book is intentionally blank!]

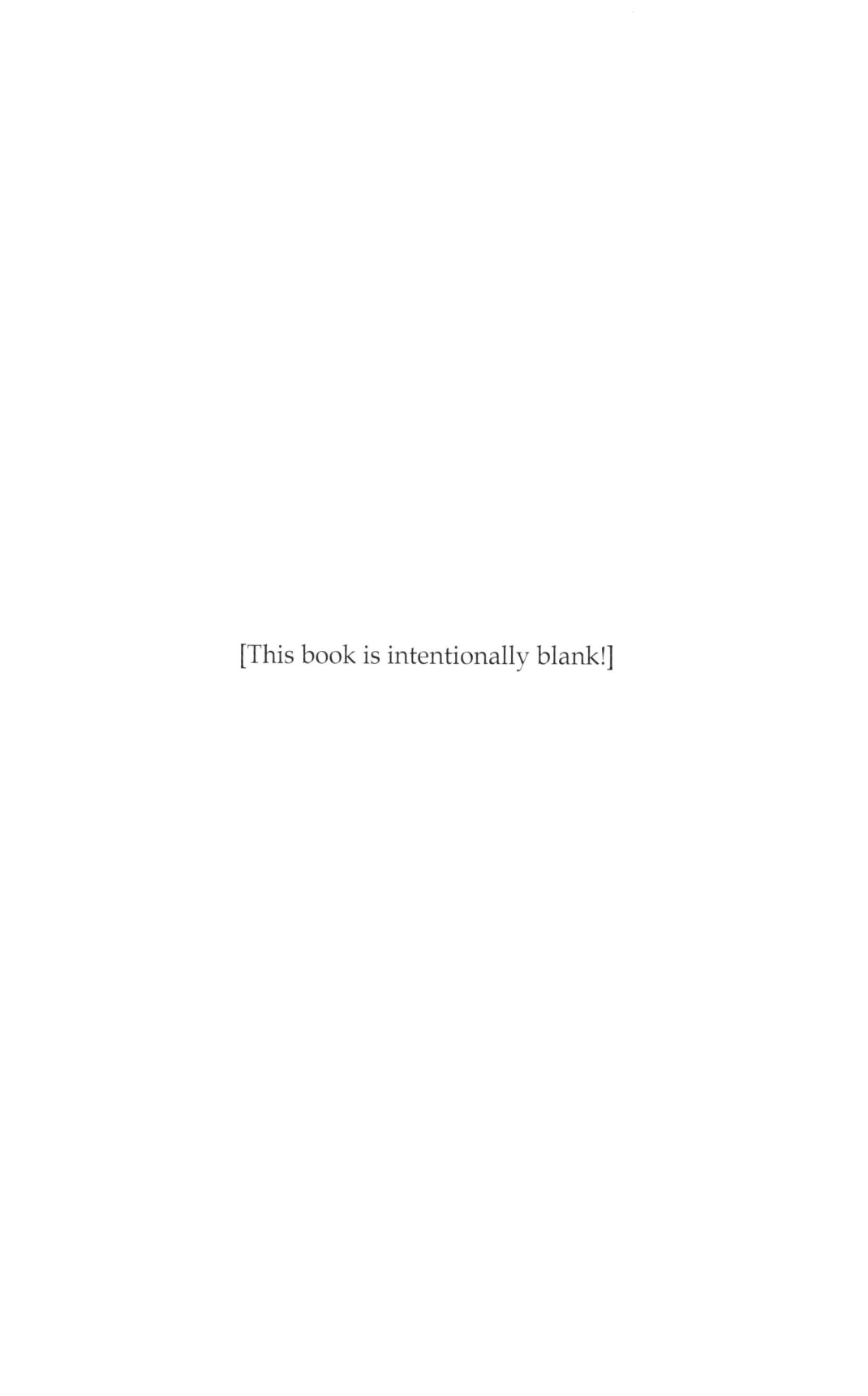

[This book is intentionally blank!]

[This book is intentionally blank!]

[This book is intentionally blank!]

[This book is intentionally blank!]

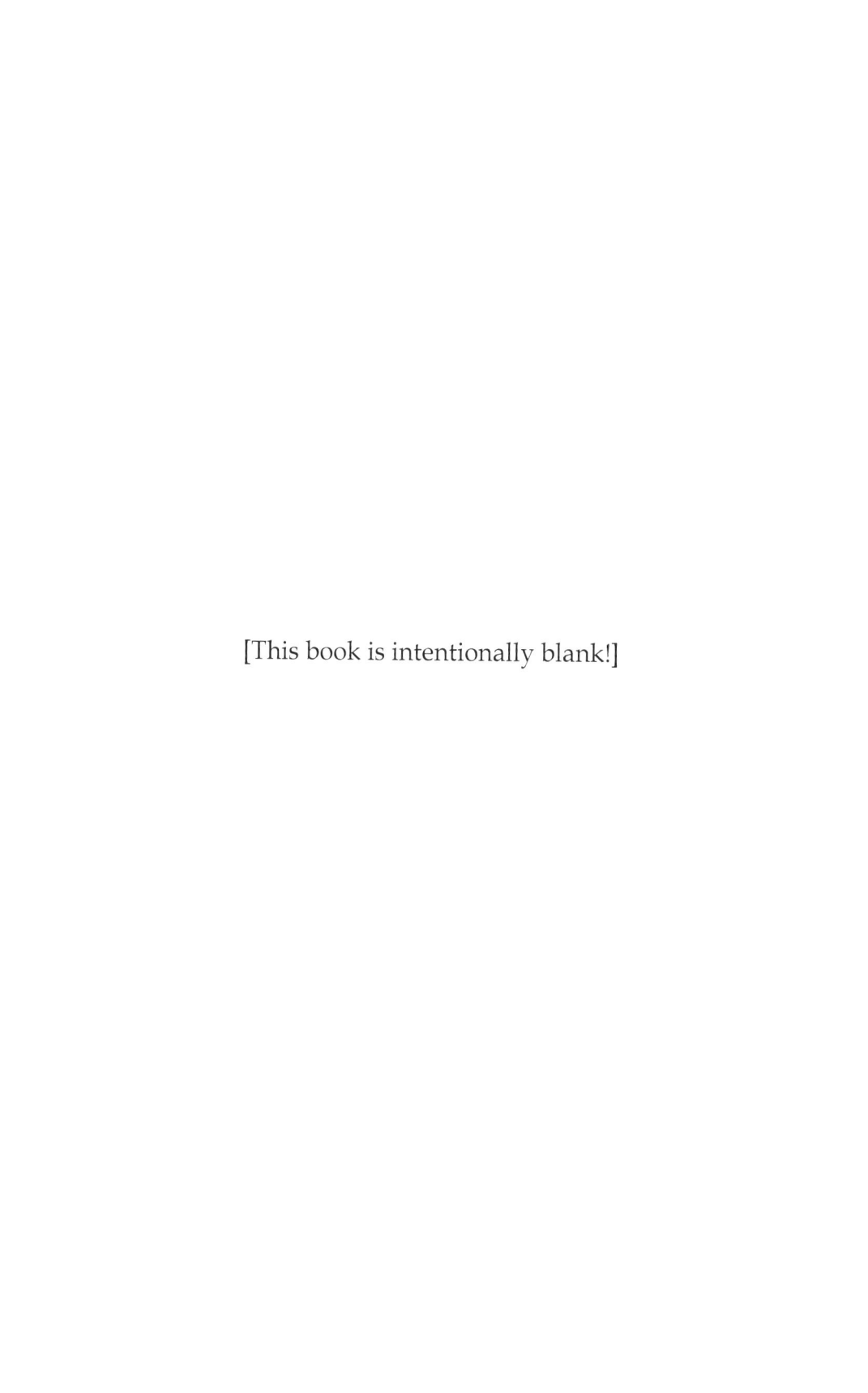

[This book is intentionally blank!]

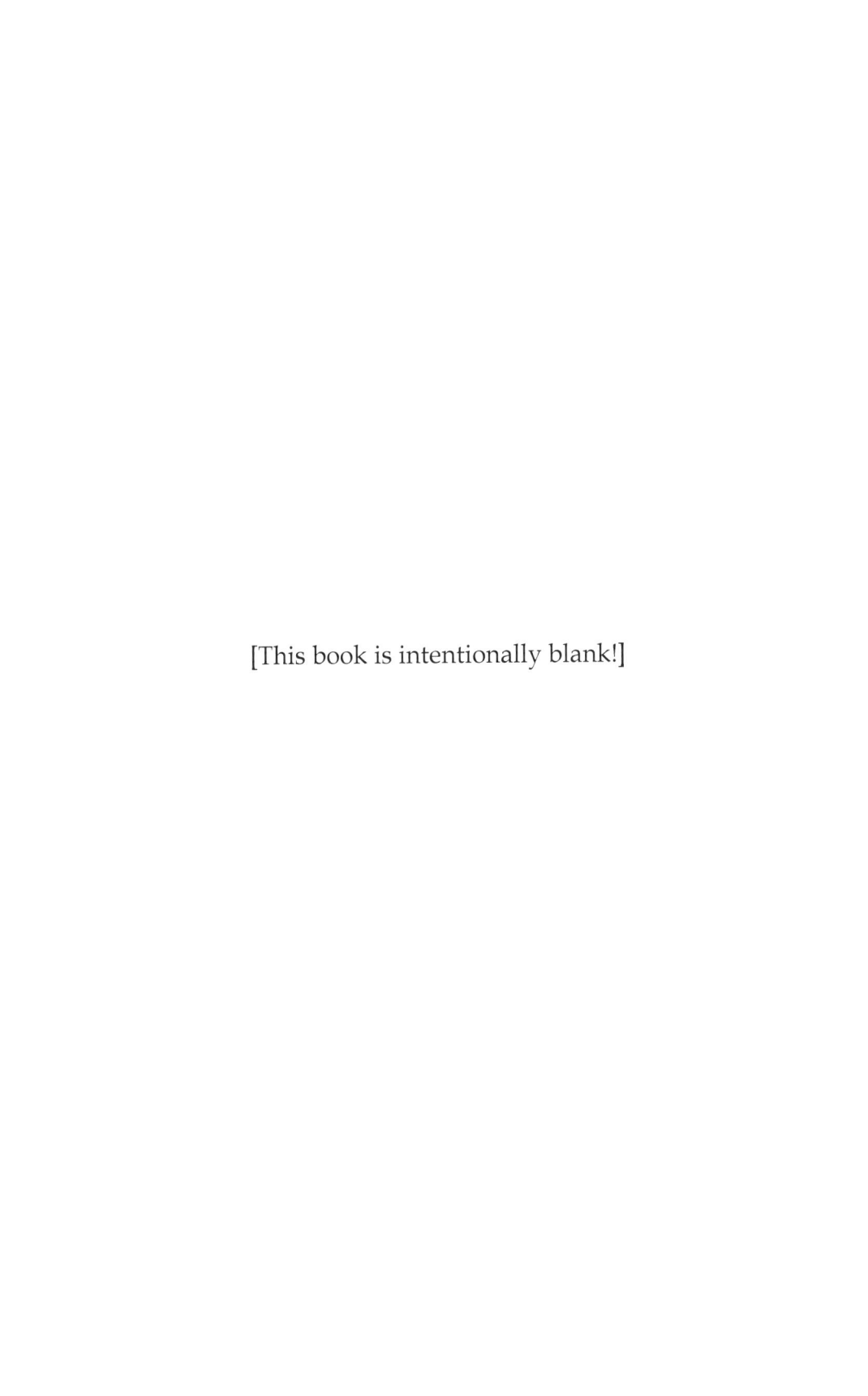

[This book is intentionally blank!]

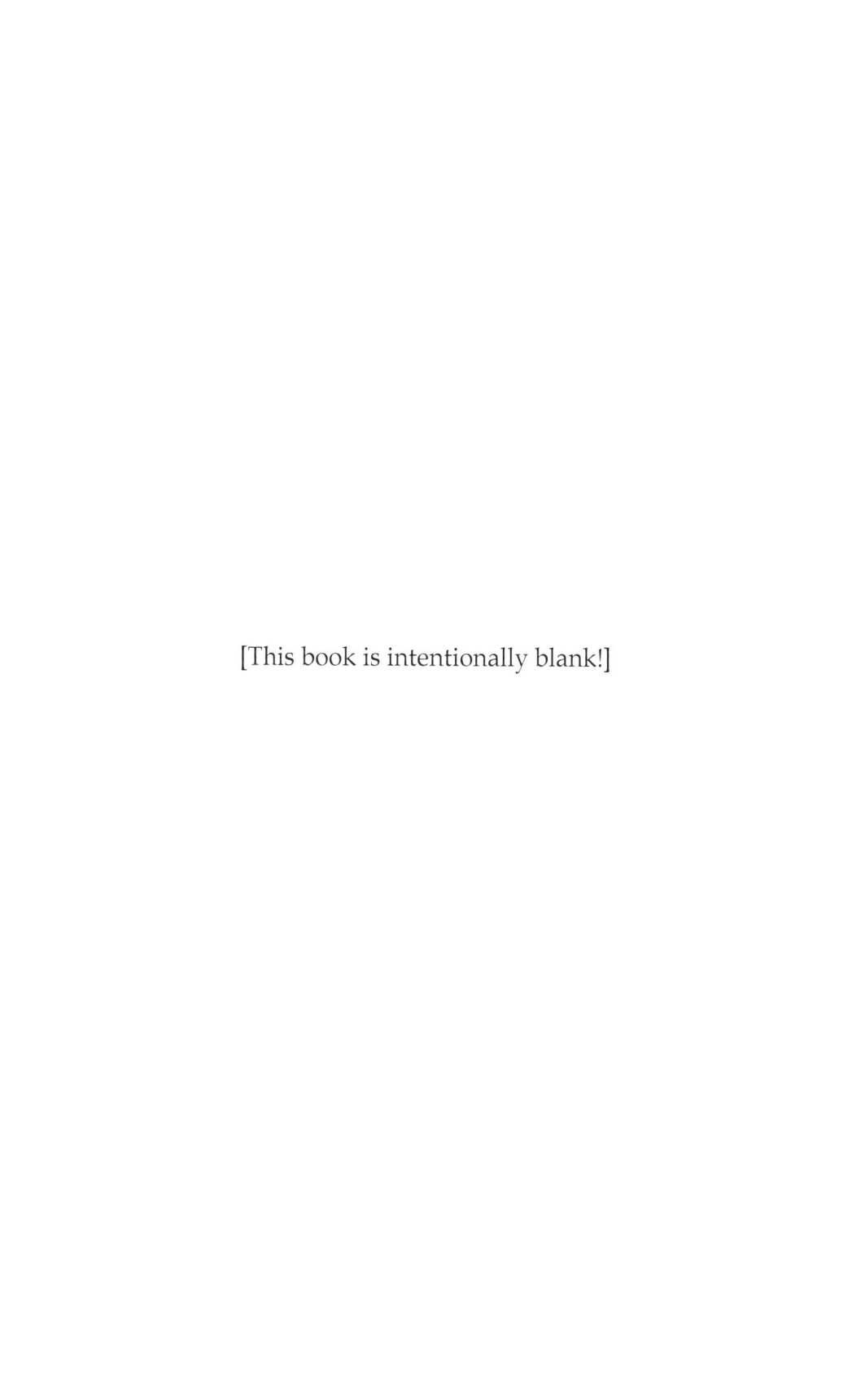

[This book is intentionally blank!]

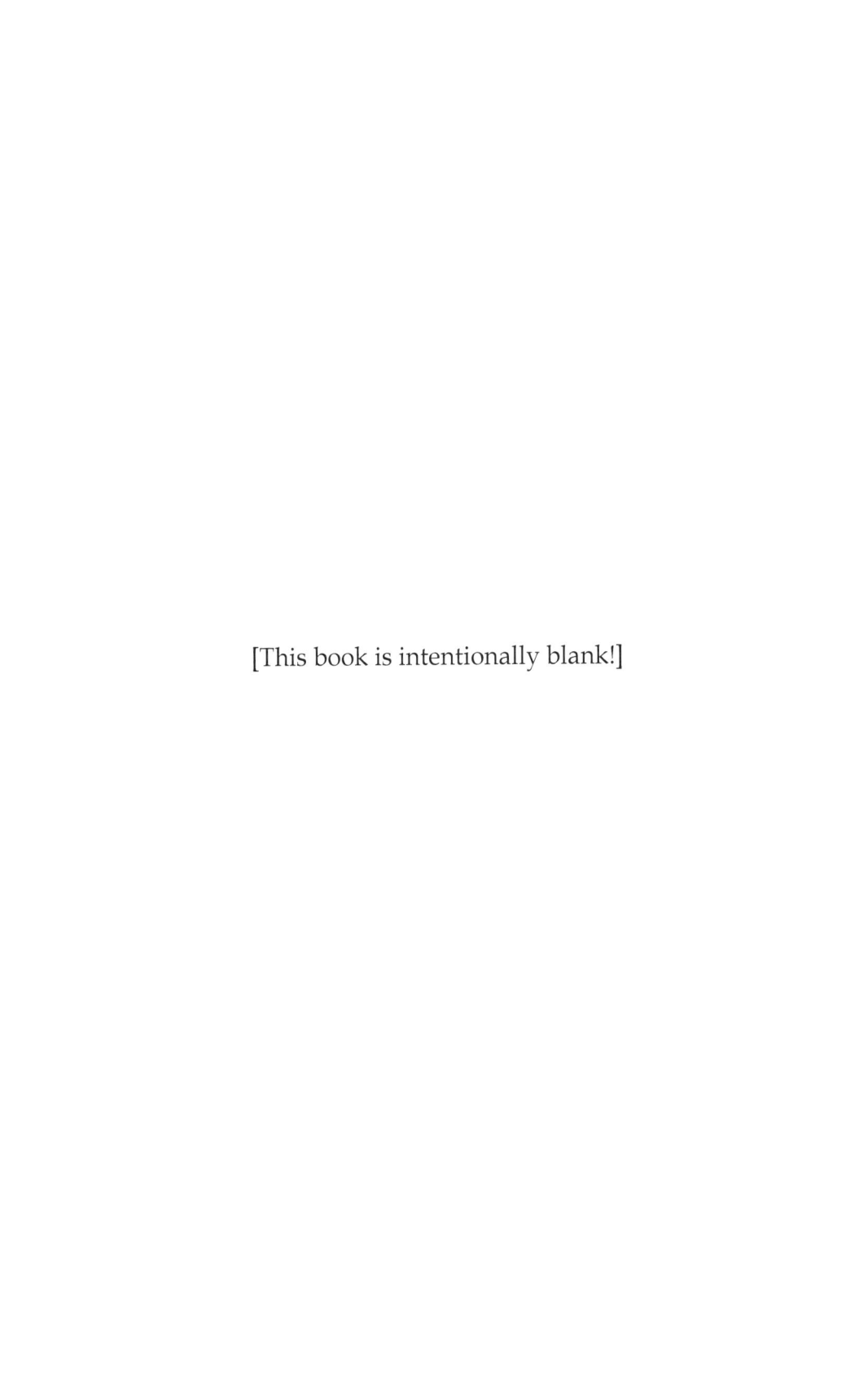

[This book is intentionally blank!]

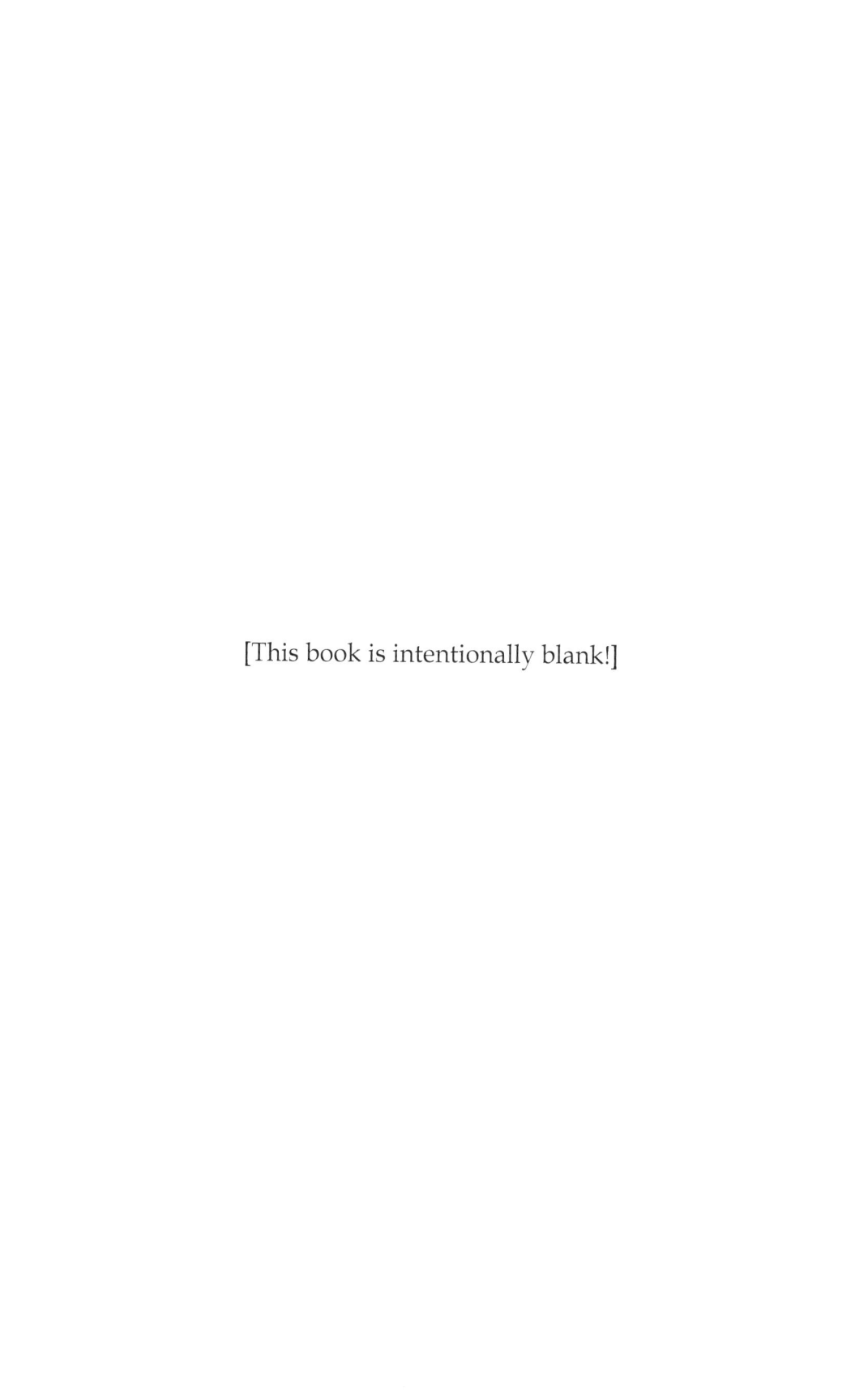

[This book is intentionally blank!]

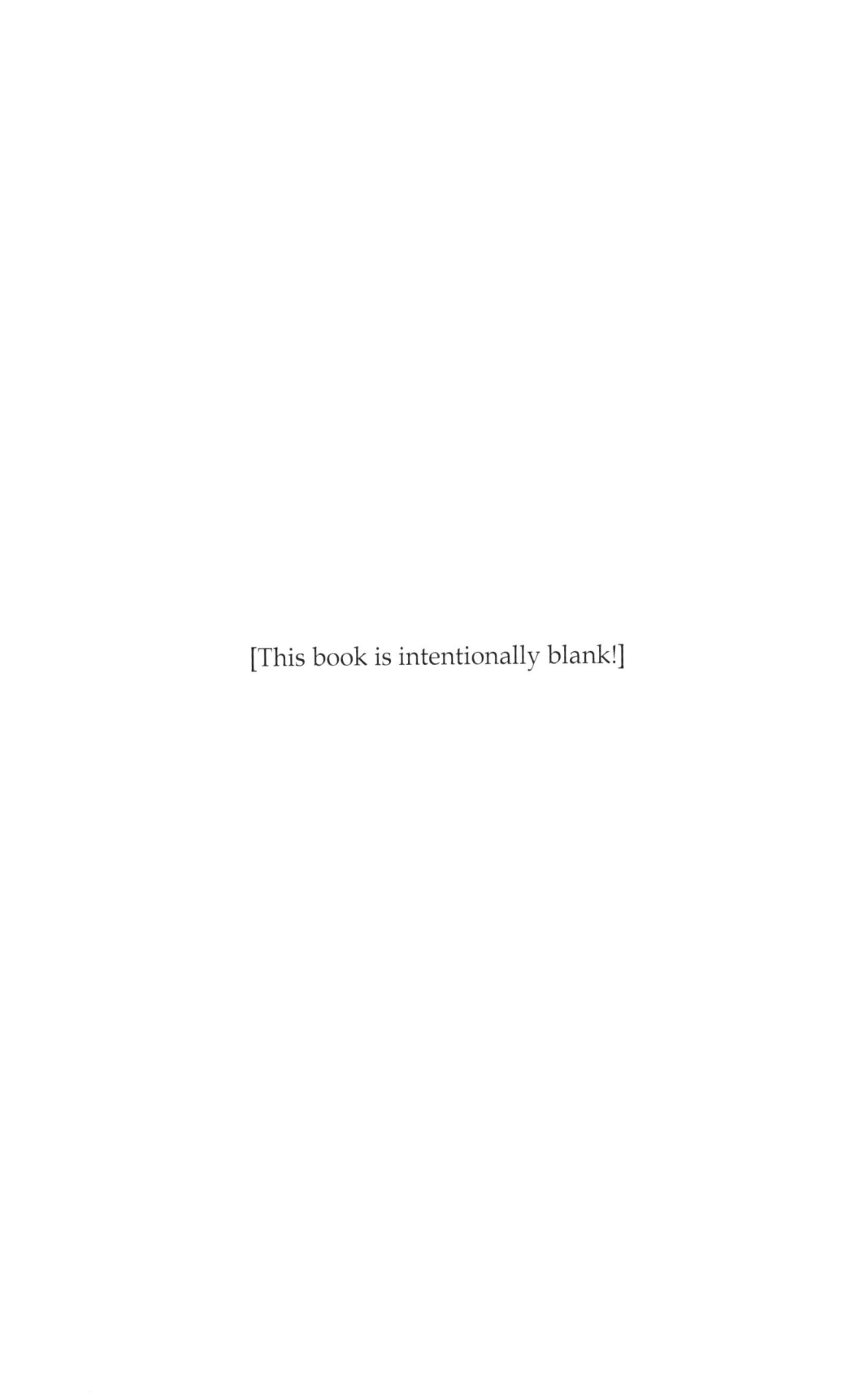

[This book is intentionally blank!]

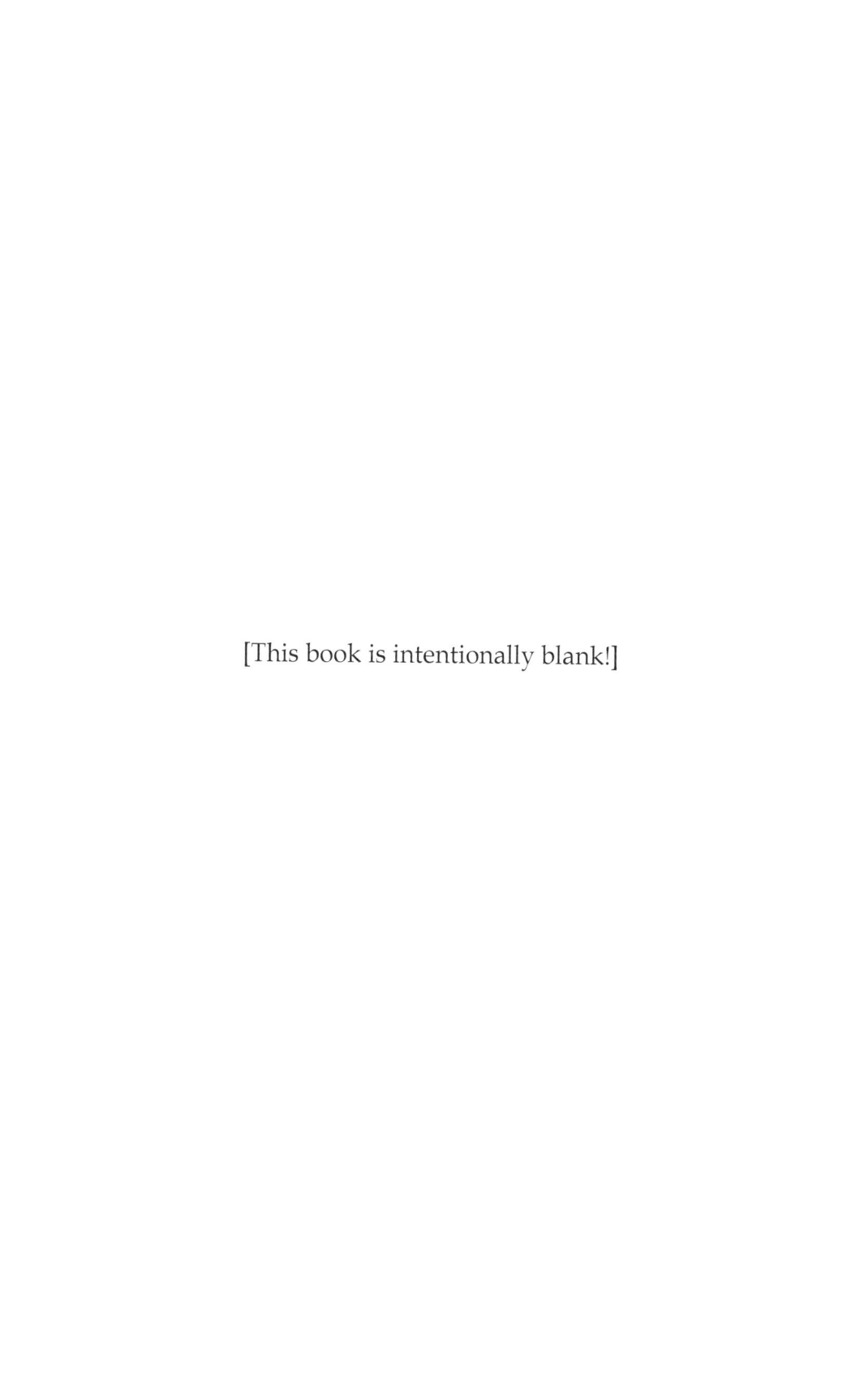

[This book is intentionally blank!]

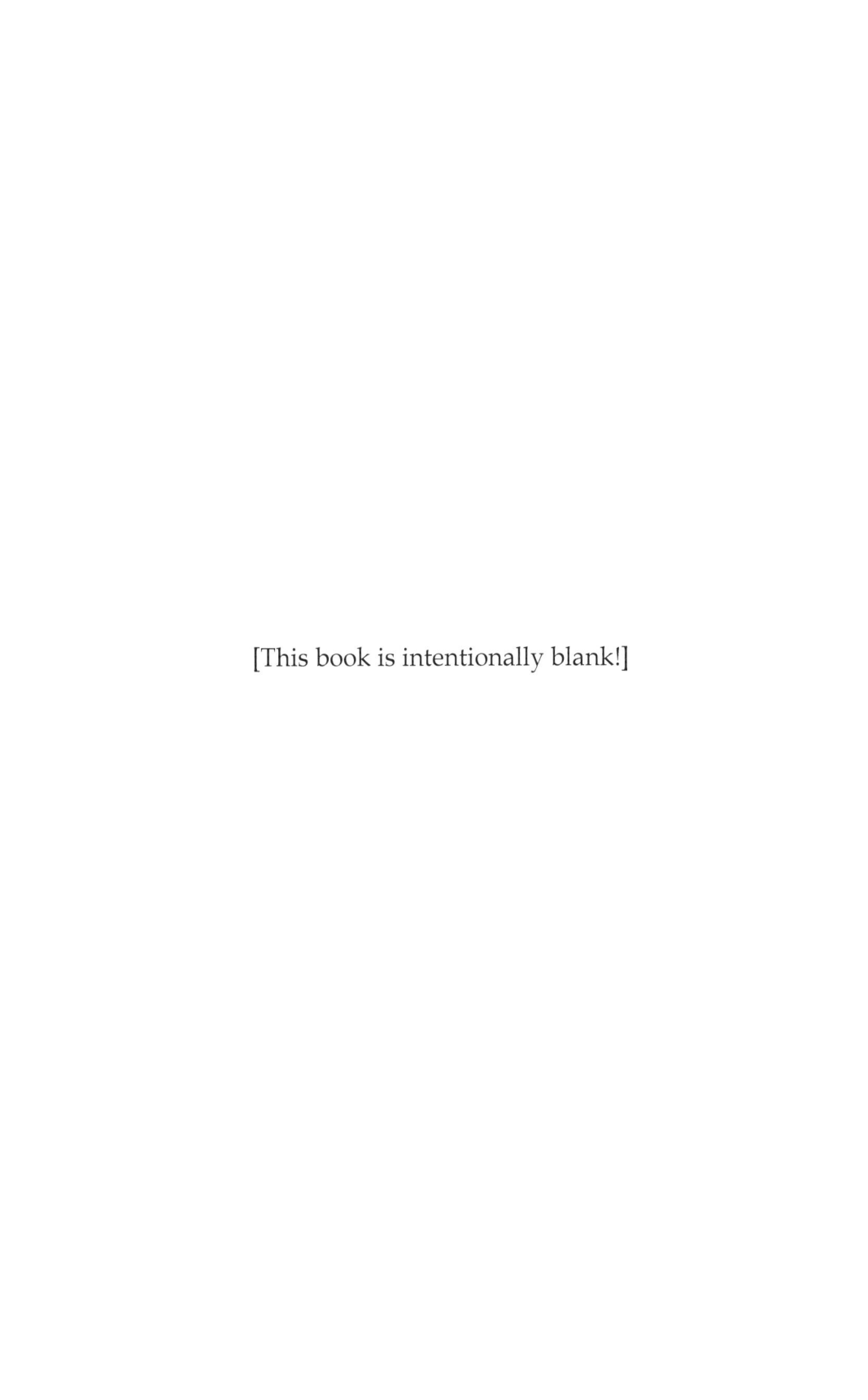

[This book is intentionally blank!]

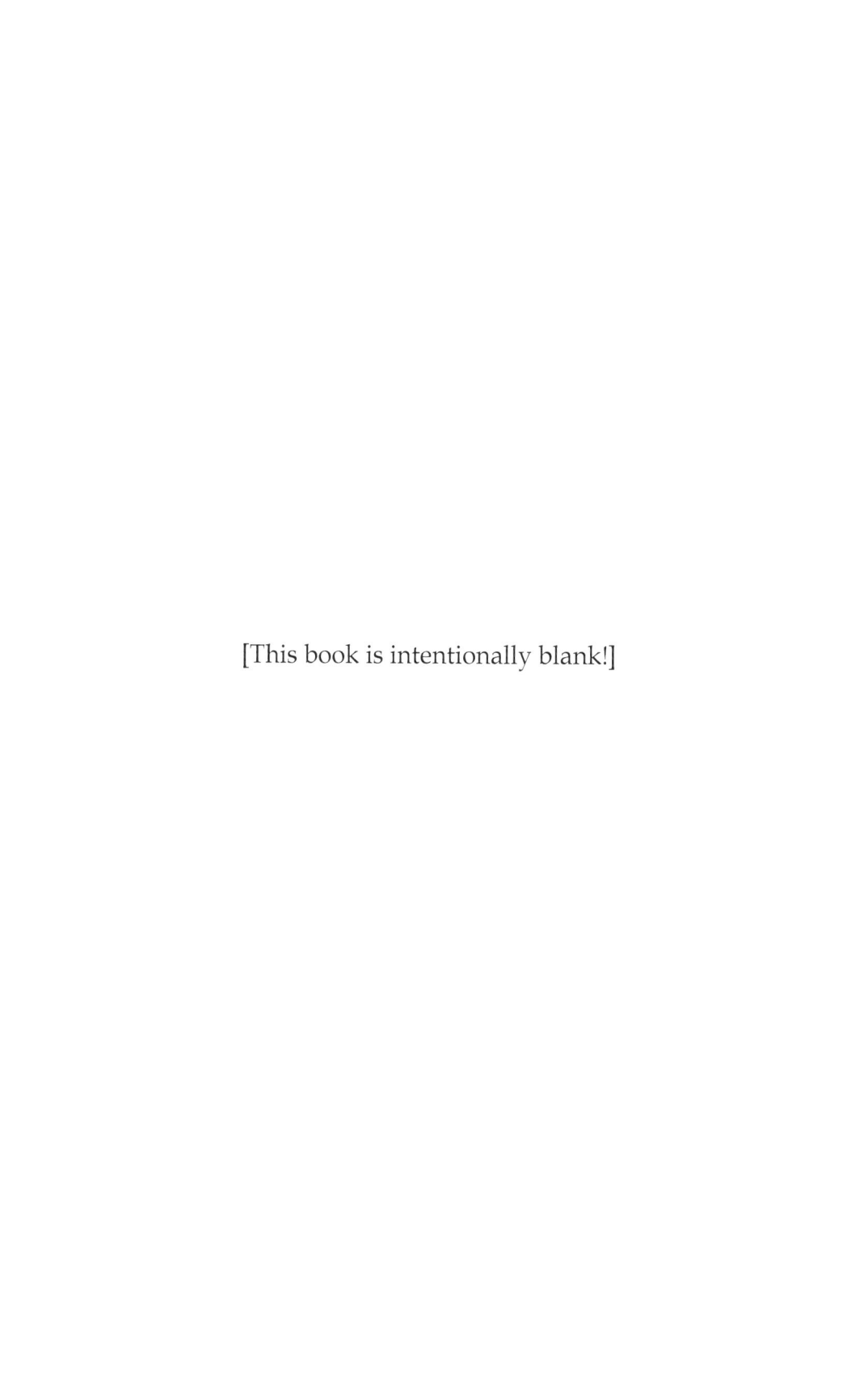

[This book is intentionally blank!]

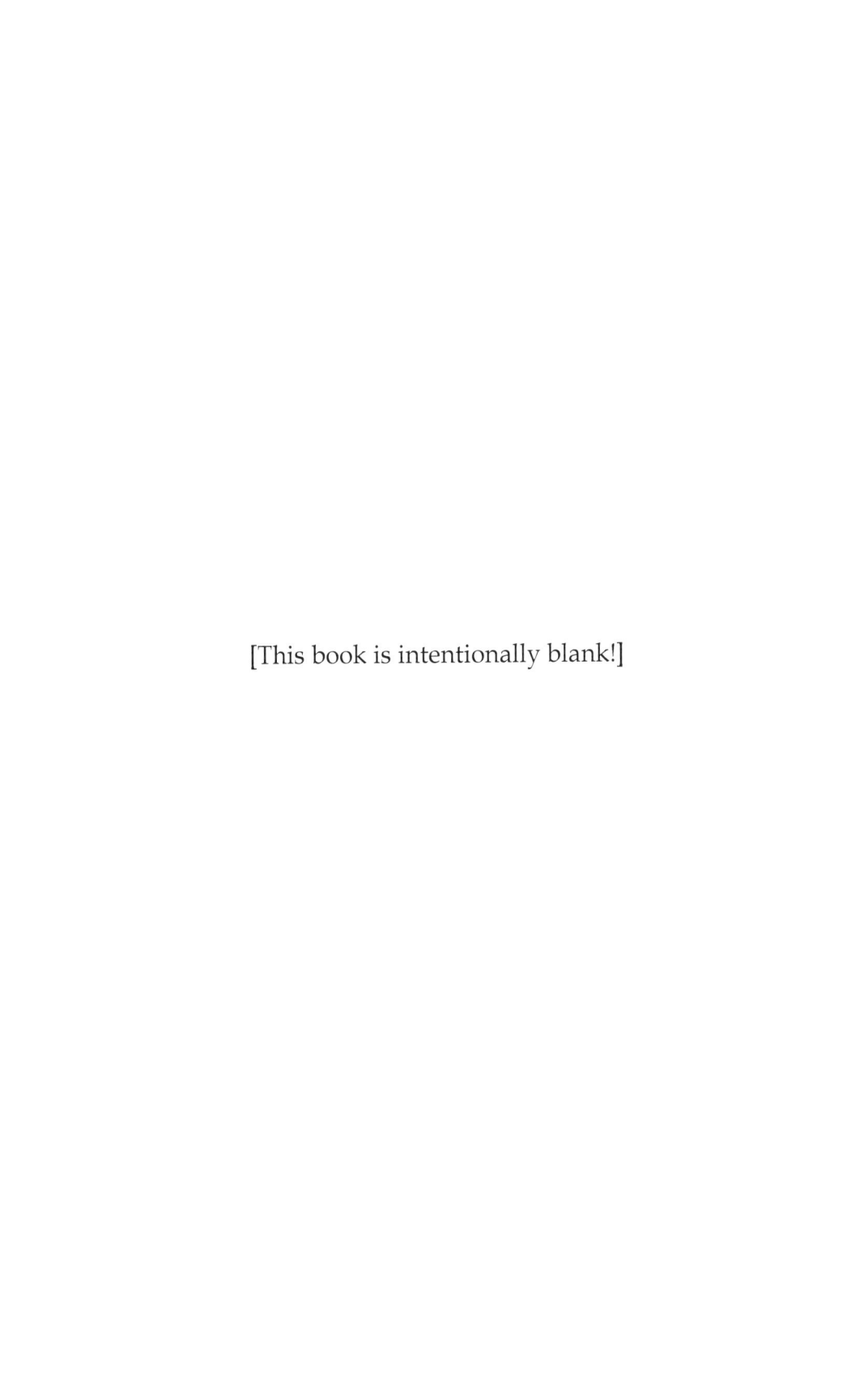

[This book is intentionally blank!]

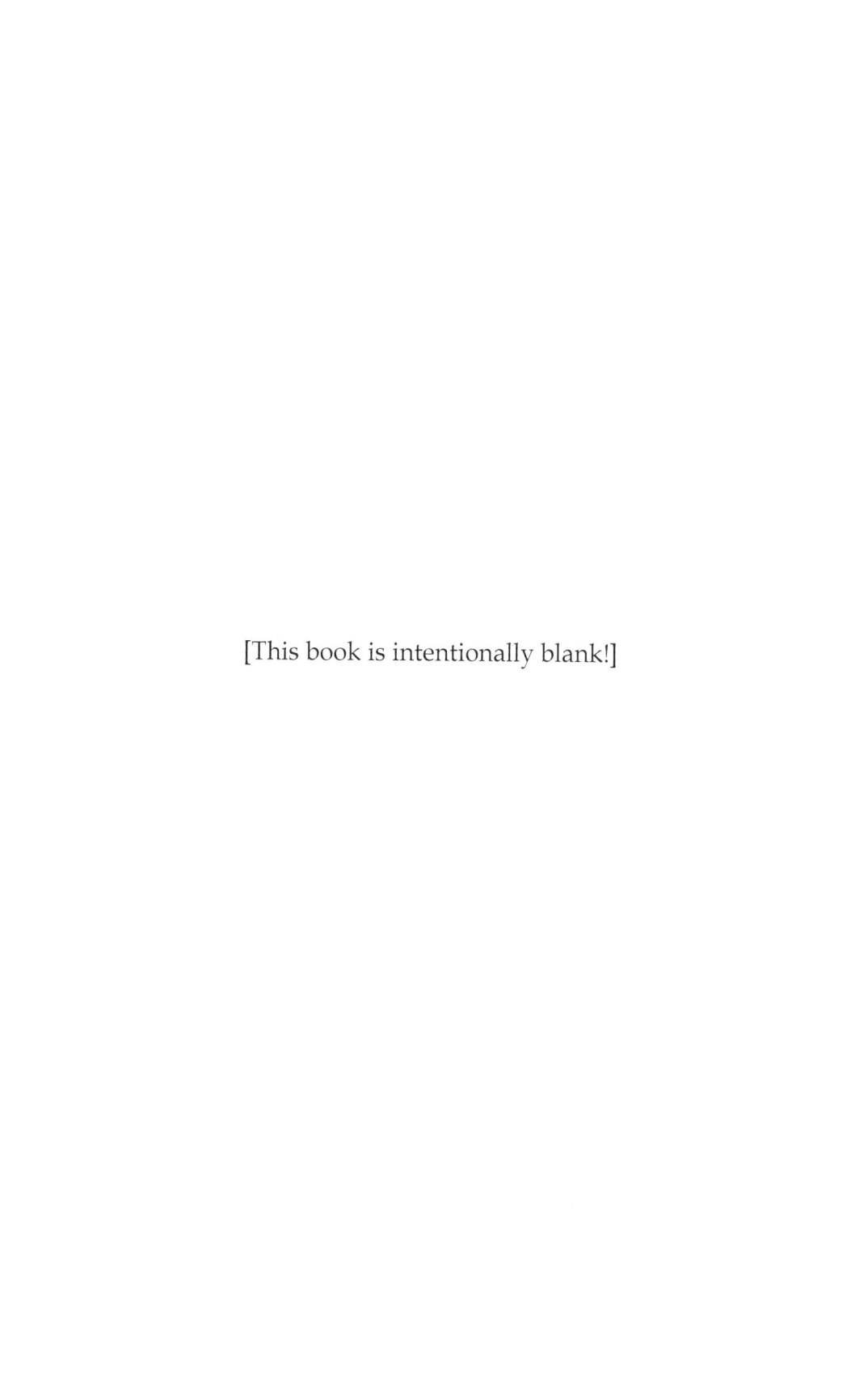

[This book is intentionally blank!]

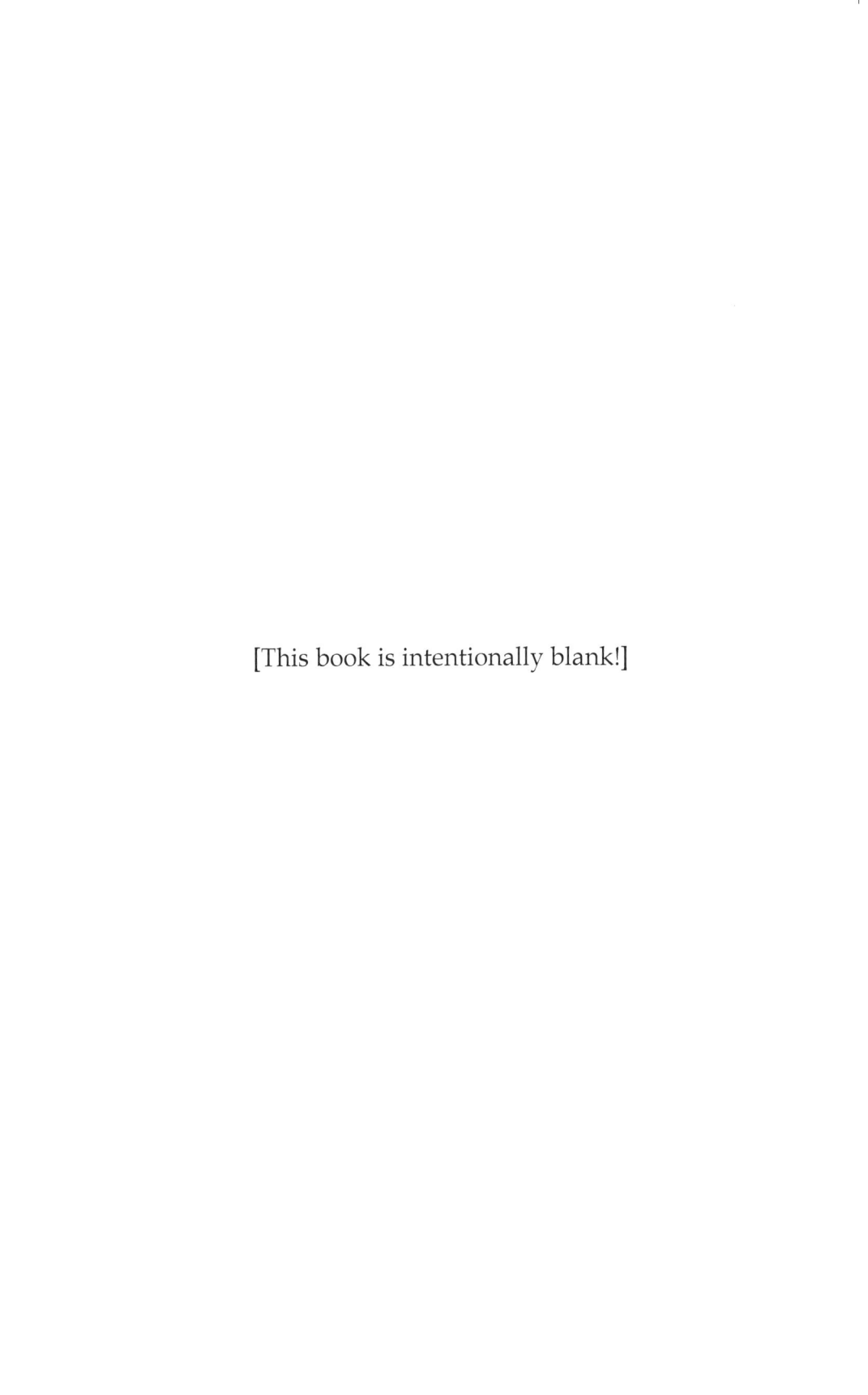

[This book is intentionally blank!]

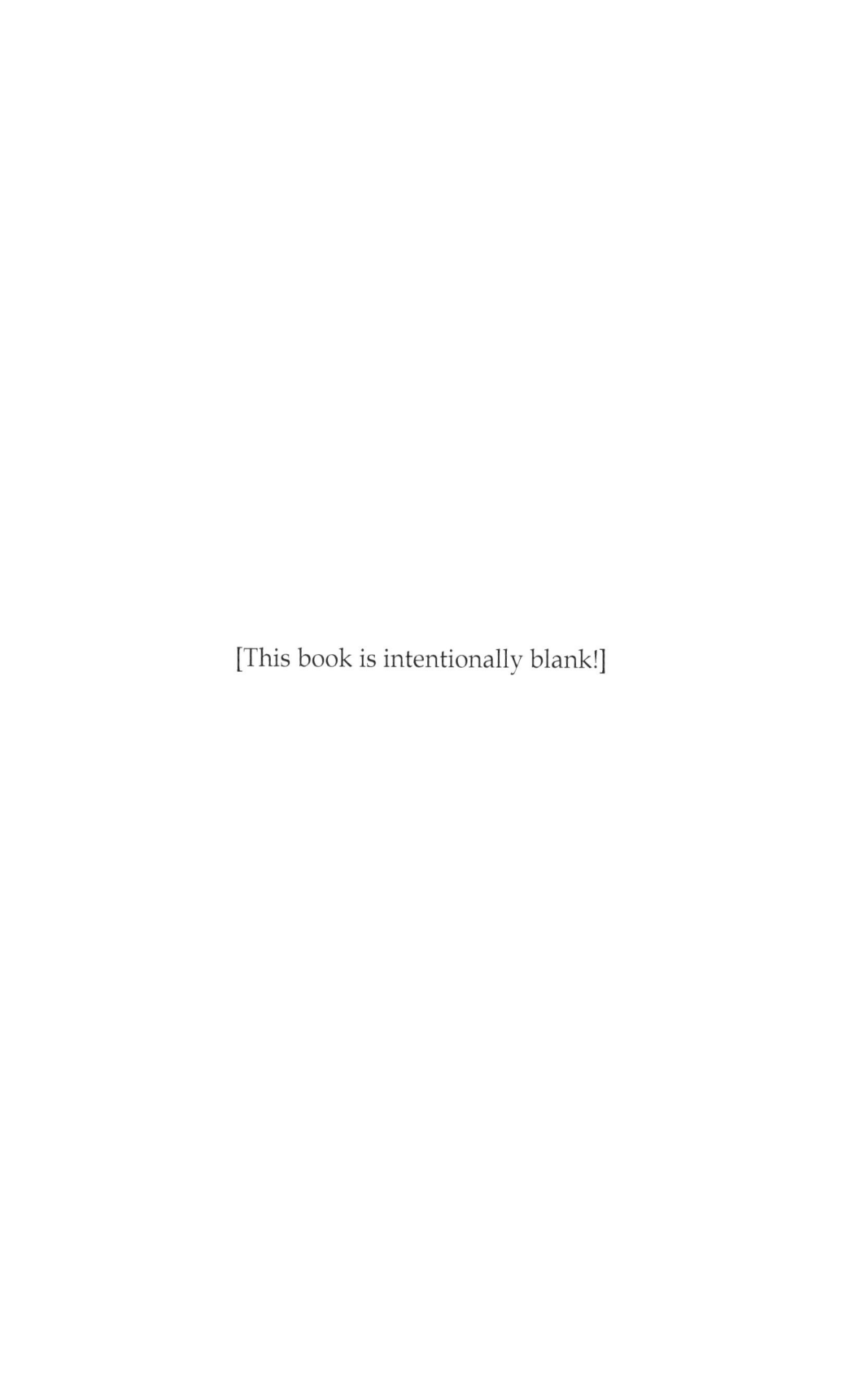

[This book is intentionally blank!]

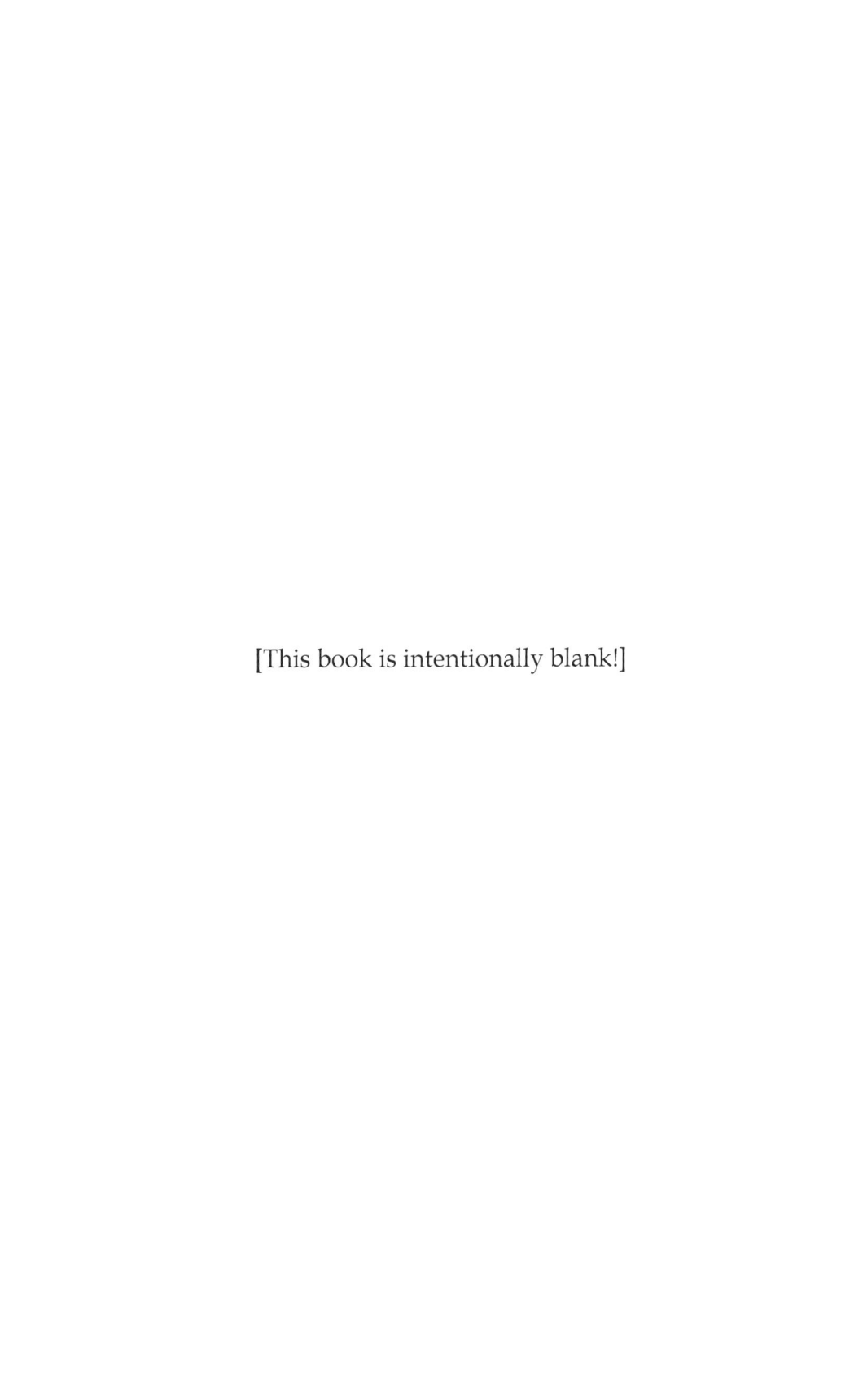

[This book is intentionally blank!]

[This book is intentionally blank!]

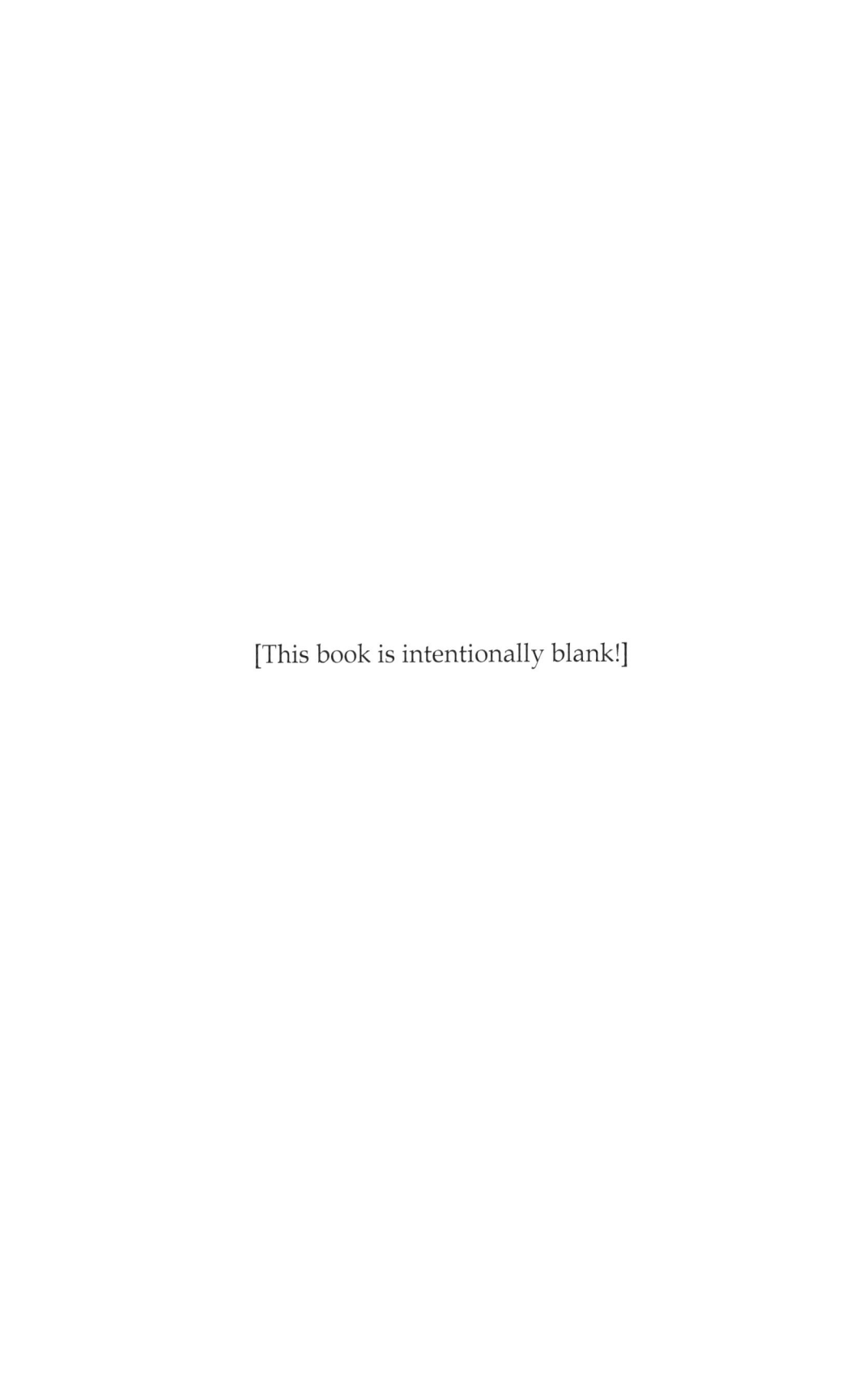

[This book is intentionally blank!]

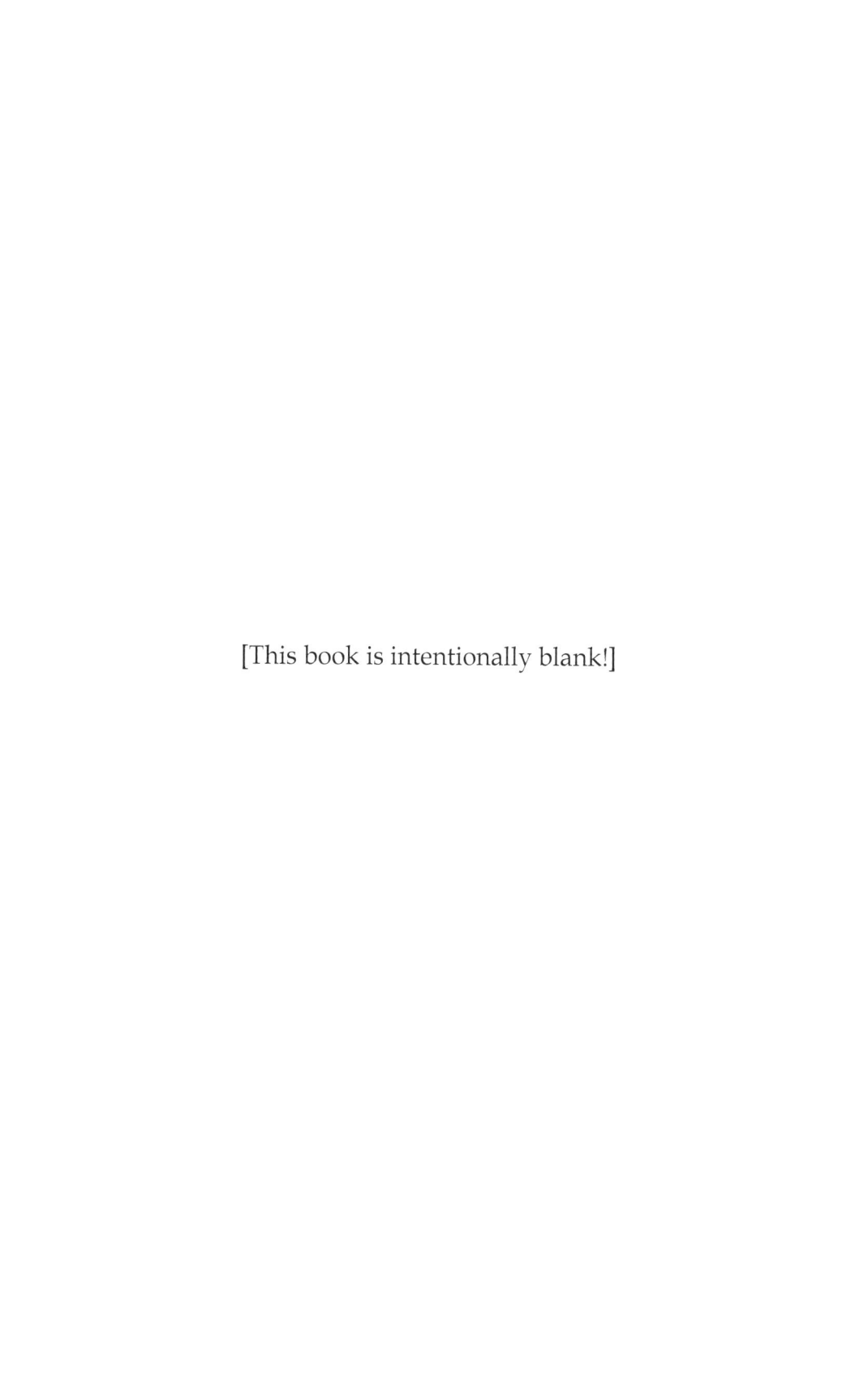

[This book is intentionally blank!]

[This book is intentionally blank!]

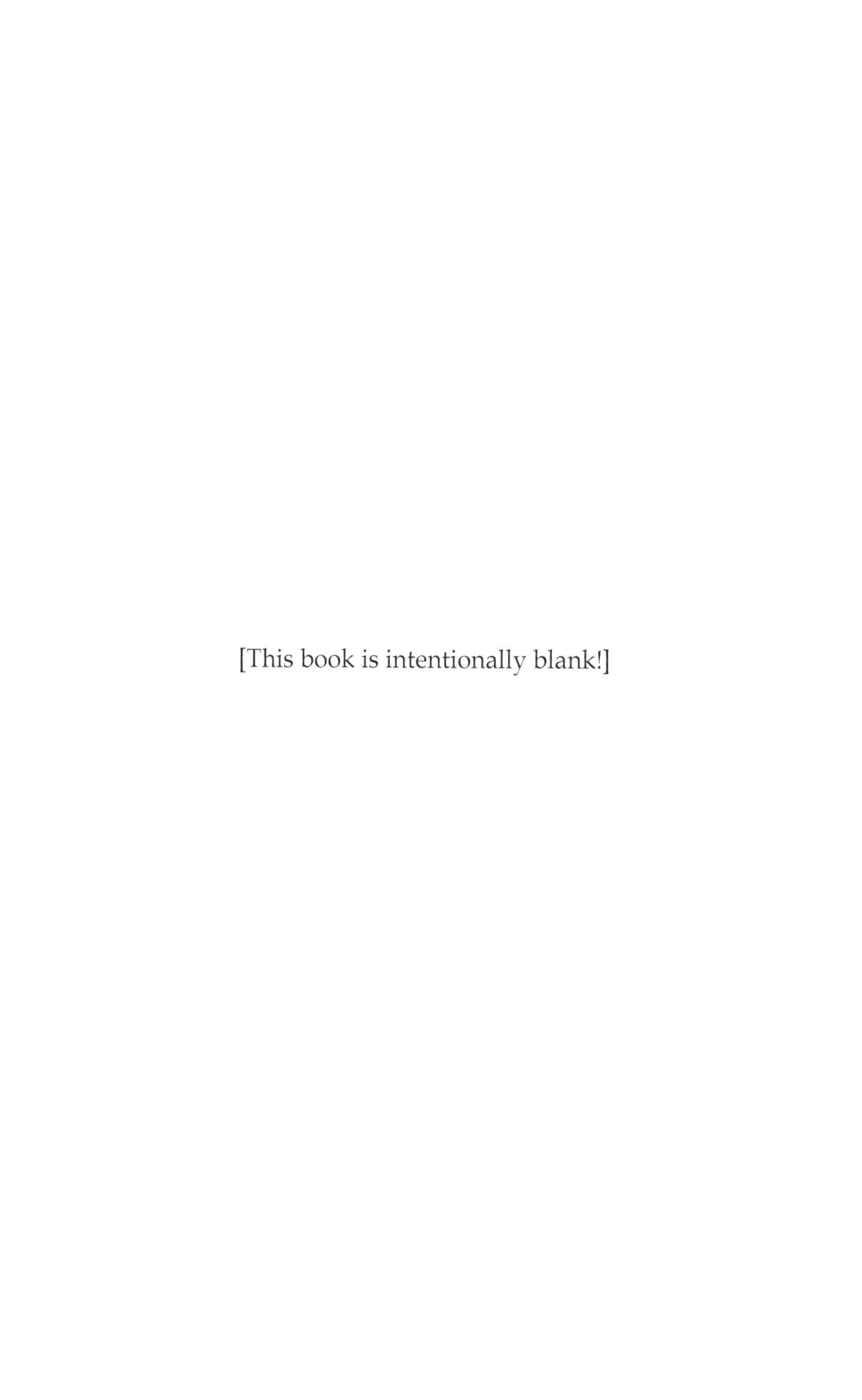

[This book is intentionally blank!]

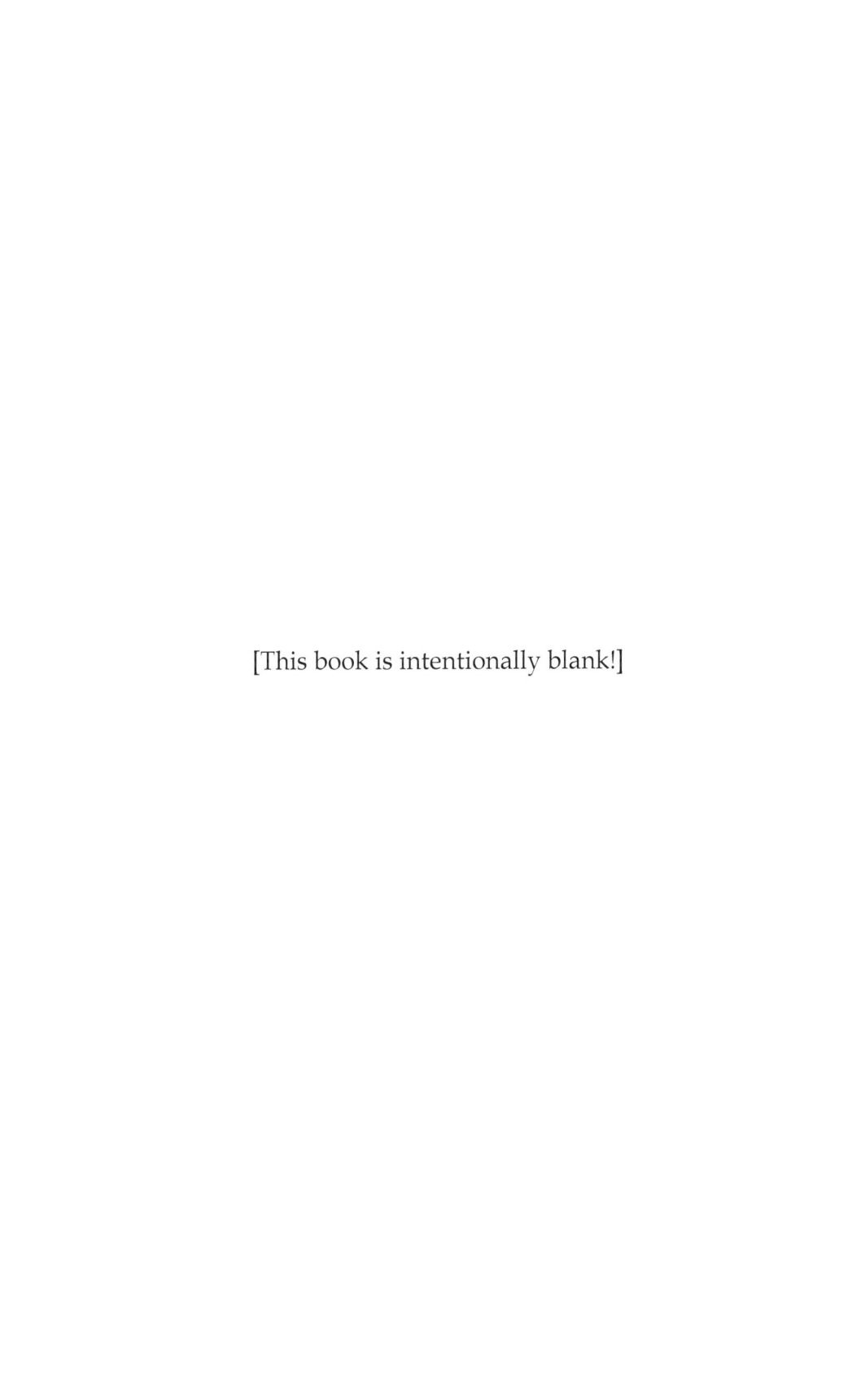

[This book is intentionally blank!]

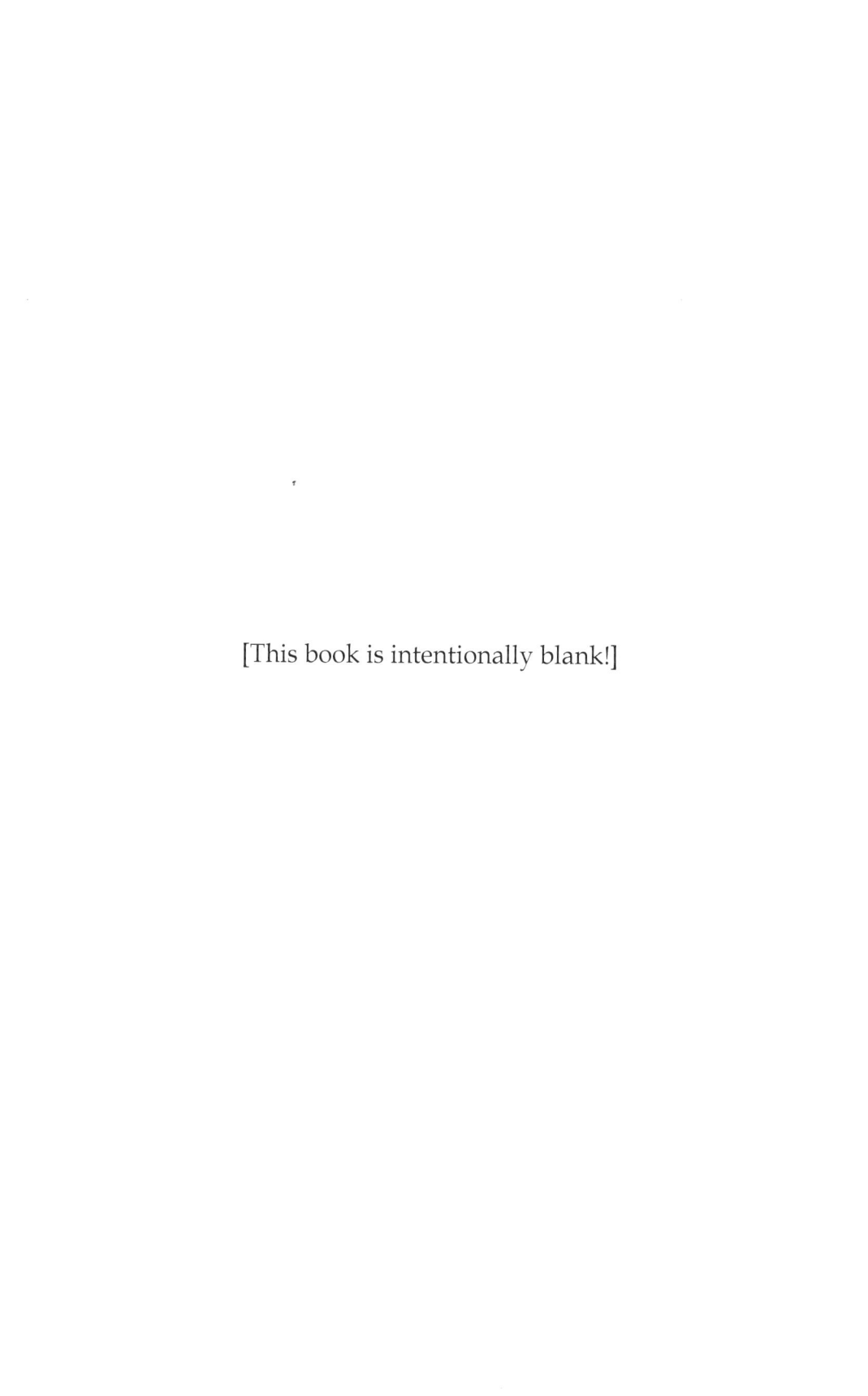

[This book is intentionally blank!]

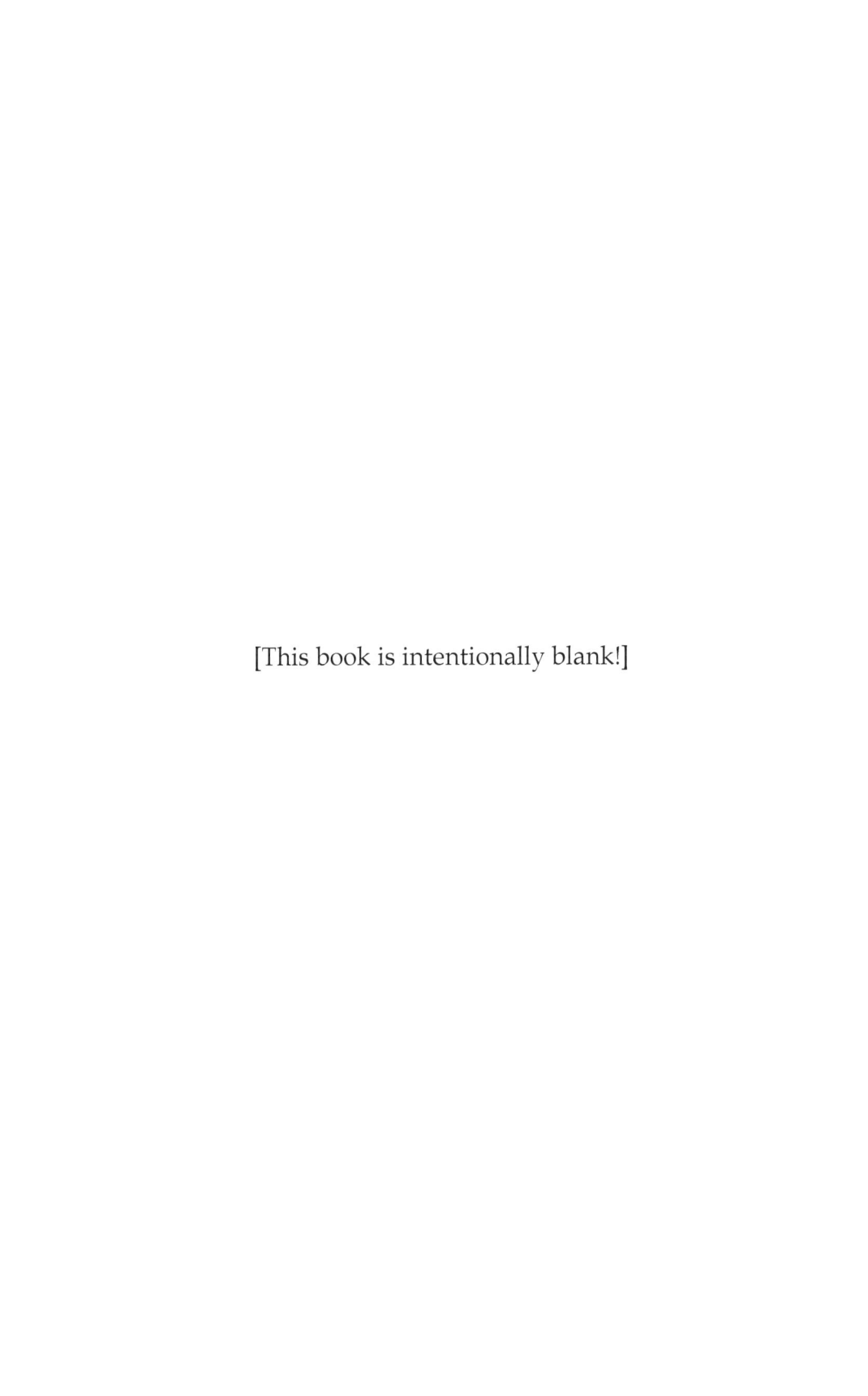

[This book is intentionally blank!]

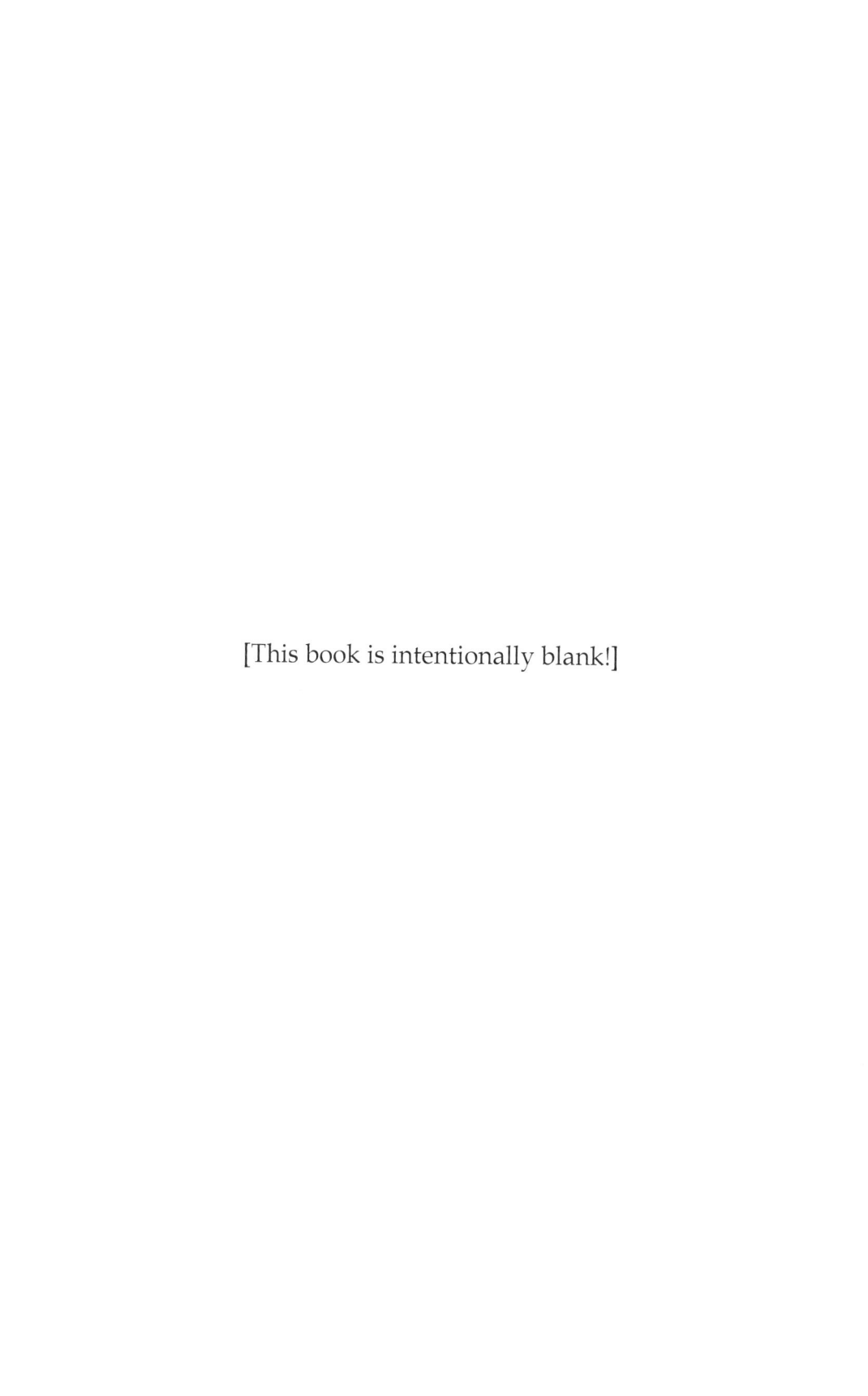

[This book is intentionally blank!]

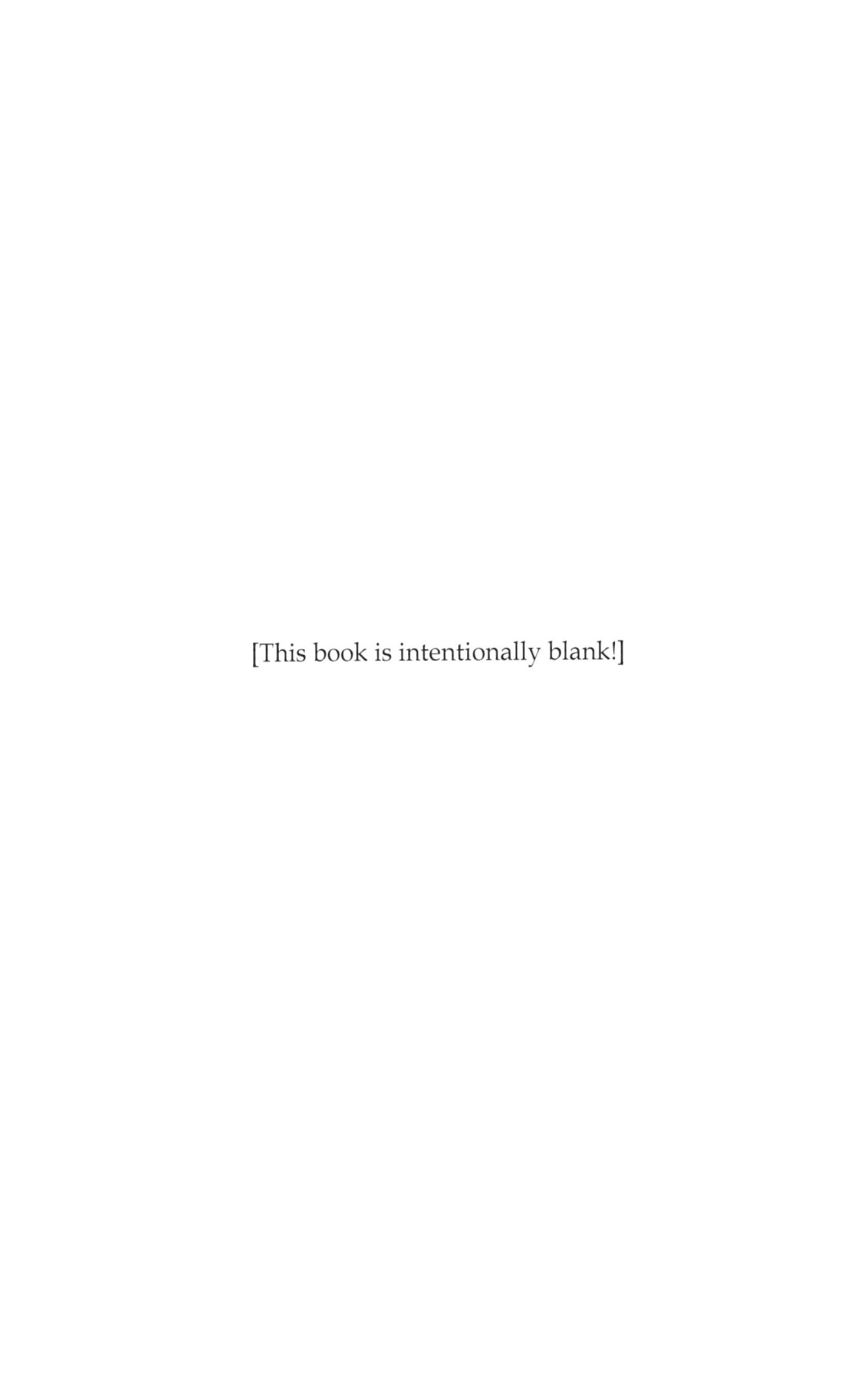

[This book is intentionally blank!]

[This book is intentionally blank!]

[This book is intentionally blank!]

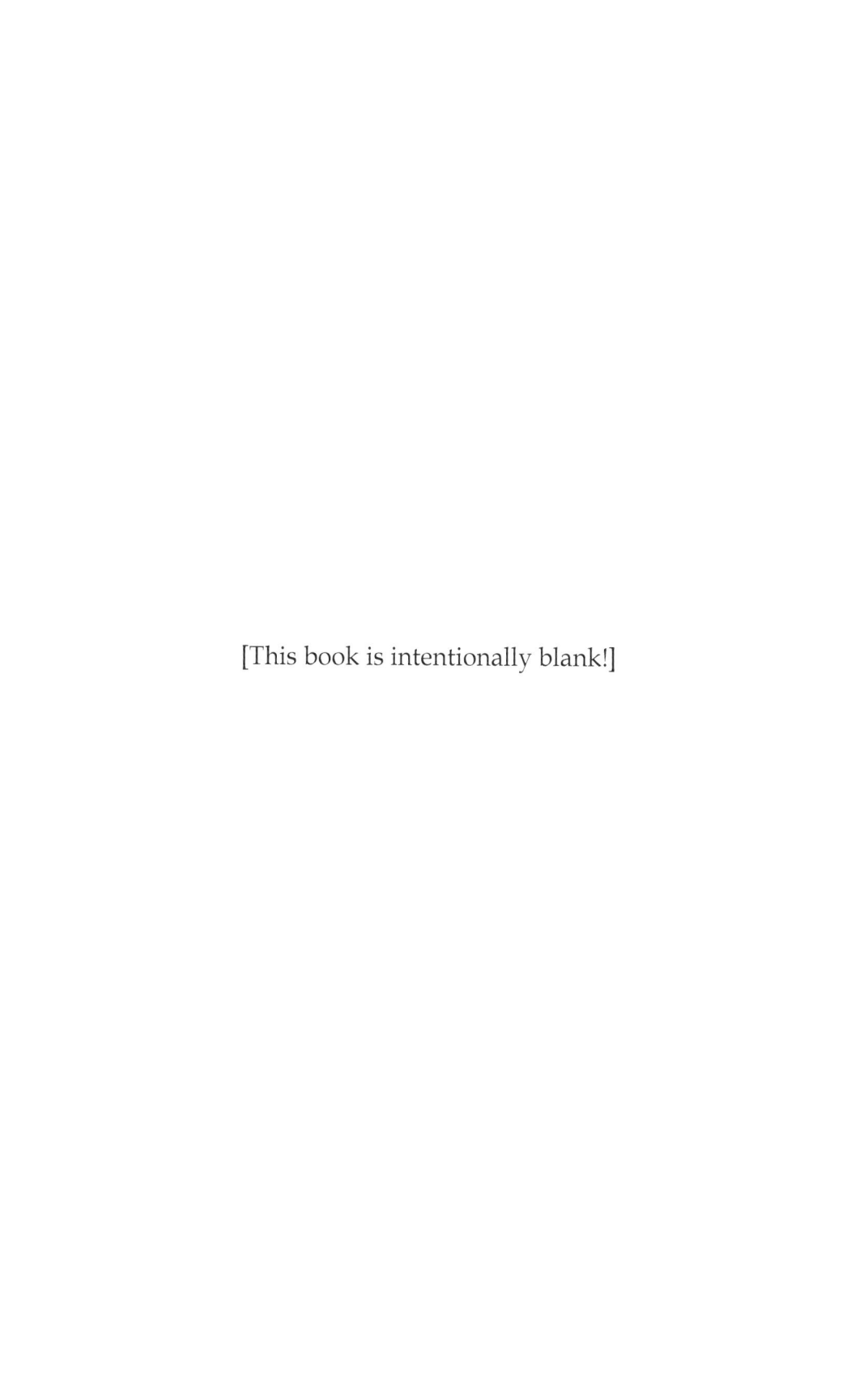

[This book is intentionally blank!]

[This book is intentionally blank!]

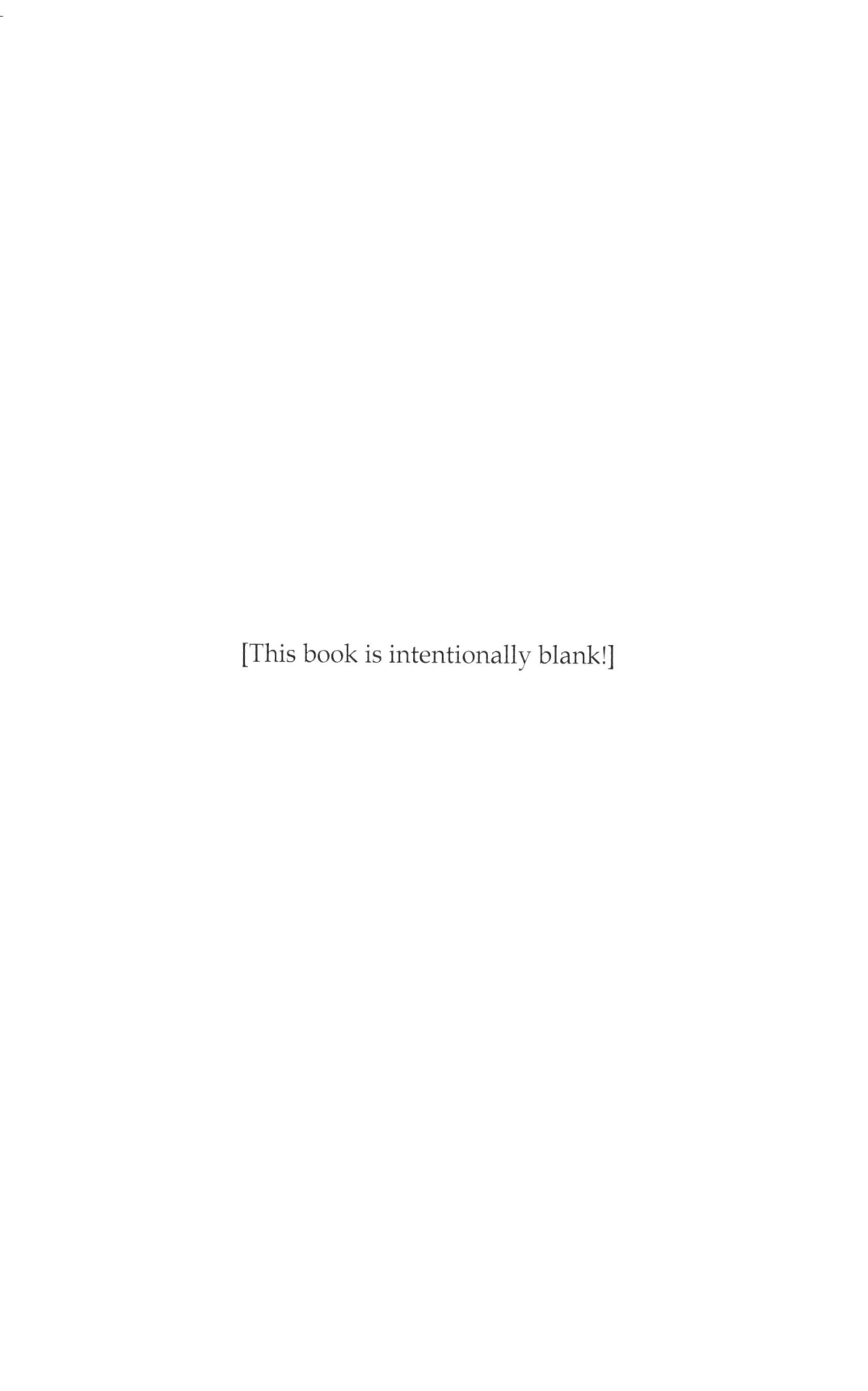

[This book is intentionally blank!]

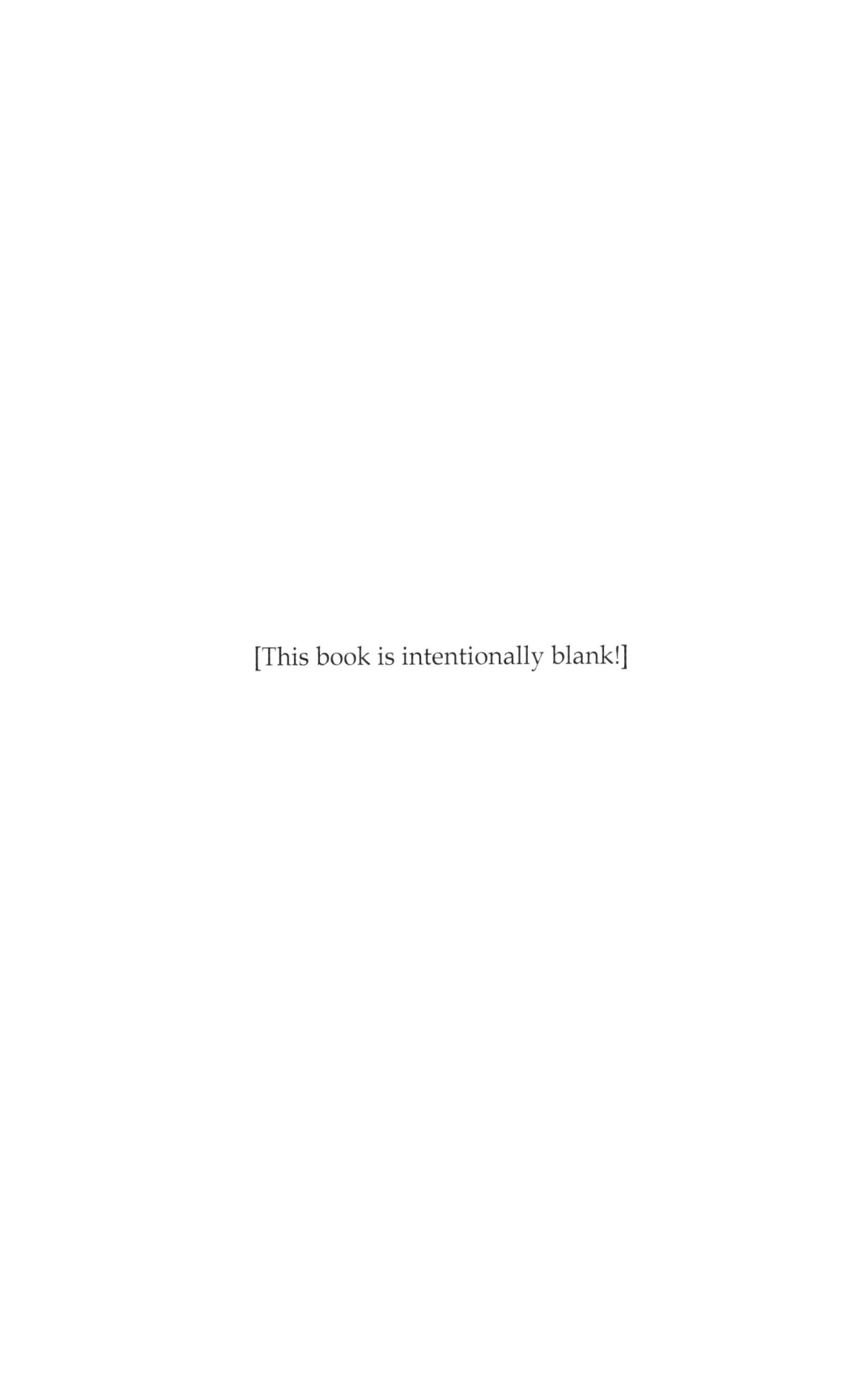

Printed in Great Britain
by Amazon